In *The Seer Anointing*, Aaron does a great job of explaining what it means to be a seer and how the gift operates. He shares his personal experiences and how he has helped others develop this gift to be a blessing to others and build up the Church. As a pastor, I often counsel people who deal with anxiety and depression issues, and it seems as though the number of people who deal with these issues is increasing. I believe many of these individuals actually possess a strong prophetic or seeing gift that they haven't learned how to use appropriately.

Marty Pronovost
Senior Pastor, LifeHouse Humboldt
Humboldt, California

One of the things about "seeing" is it is impossible to unsee. The responsibility to properly steward what one has seen is a test that very few seem to pass. Aaron Peterson sees, and I believe it's because he has guarded this gift so well that God has favored him with the wisdom to write about it. If you have any skepticism about prophetic ministry or the seer anointing this book probably won't dissuade your unbelief, but I can say that you will be enlightened by the insight Aaron possesses and the clarity with which he presents it. If you ever have the honor of visiting with Aaron, you'll understand what I mean. You'll understand that he is a powerfully sincere, remarkably intelligent, and thoroughly God-saturated brother who is more than secure in his identity and gifting. He is clear that both come from Christ alone, and just as he has freely received Aaron freely gives the revelation that you too can experience the gifts of God.

Bill Vanderbush
Executive Pastor, Community Presbyterian Church
Celebration, Florida
Co-Author of *The Forgotten Way*

In the Body of Christ, we all too often miss out on God's work because it goes beyond what our minds can comprehend. We read about seers in the Old Testament, and I have even heard very popular mainstream teachers mention them while reading Old Testament Scriptures. Yet, for one reason or another, there is very little actual teaching on the seer anointing. Some believers are perhaps even skeptical of it. The world today seems to be fascinated with the supernatural and spiritual realm. Just look at our movies and TV shows! While many of these glorify "the dark side" of the spiritual realm, the Church has access to the real thing as God intended! The only problem is, not all of us recognize it.

In *The Seer Anointing*, Aaron Peterson clearly articulates the "what" and the "why" behind this spiritual gift and presents a compelling case for how it can benefit the Church today. This is not just a Charismatic or Pentecostal gifting, but a way that God is working today across denominational lines. As a member of a Southern Baptist congregation, I found great value in this book! I recently heard a fellow minister say, "We don't get to curate the way God reveals Himself to us." It is true; we cannot reject aspects of God that we see in Scripture simply because they are not part of our tradition or experience. I urge those who are skeptical to read *The Seer Anointing* and embrace the complete work of God in their lives.

JARED STUMP
Executive Director, Life Impact Ministries
Author of *Creation & Redemption:*
Finding Your Place in a Fallen World and *Identity in Christ*

THE
SEER
ANOINTING

RESTORING AN ANCIENT GIFT TO THE MODERN CHURCH

AARON J. PETERSON

BATTLE GROUND
creative

THE SEER ANOINTING

Copyright © 2018 by Aaron Peterson

Published in Houston, Texas, by Battle Ground Creative
First Edition

ISBN 978-0-9908738-9-1
RELIGION / Christian Life / Spiritual Growth

Battle Ground Creative is a publishing company with an emphasis on helping first-time authors find their voice. Named after an obscure city in Washington State, we currently operate offices in Houston, Texas, and Philadelphia, Pennsylvania. For a complete title list and bulk order information, please visit www.battlegroundcreative.com.

Scripture taken from the NEW AMERICAN STANDARD BIBLE®, Copyright © 1960,1962,1963,1968,1971,1972,1973,1975,1977,1995 by The Lockman Foundation. Used by permission.

Senior copyeditor: Jared Stump
Cover design: Corinne Karl
Cover image: Lightstock
Author photo: Ruthanna Tepp
Interior design and typeset: Katherine Lloyd

Printed in the United States of America

For Serenity.
Drink deep, my little seer.

CONTENTS

FOREWORD

By Ryan Kibbe

I will never forget the day a young man in his late 20's or early 30's approached me right after the service. I could tell he had something to say. Maybe he had a question or concern about the message? I didn't know him at all. He appeared to have something serious on his mind, and it wasn't long before he let it rip.

"I saw what looked like a large bowl over your congregation. I saw an angel pouring oil out above this bowl covering the entire sanctuary, and it's leaking through holes in the bowl onto the people."

I was polite as I began to process what I just heard. I thanked him for sharing, but I wasn't quite sure in the moment what God was up to. Little did I know.

Now, if you are reading this book, then this story probably peeks your curiosity. As the pastor of a new church plant in Green Bay, Wisconsin, I can assure you that all kinds of people bring forth all kinds of words. Some are of the Lord, and some are not. So, I prayed about it. I conferred with other trusted leaders. Somehow, I knew this word was of God. This was what God was doing. The bowl represented a religious filter that was prohibiting His people from receiving the oil, representing the love and power God wants to pour out on His church—the anointing.

This vision celebrated the inroads God was making, chipping away at the barriers. It stirred in me a desire to see that entire bowl collapse under the weight of His glory. It was the right word, at the right time, in the right season—for our church and for me personally. The young man who brought me this word was a brilliant young theologian and seer named Aaron Peterson.

Over the next year, I kept in contact with Aaron while he was attending ministry school in California. You might say, in a sense, the Lord had me "stalk" him and his wife, Cally. We had many phone conversations from 2014 to 2015 and it became clear that Aaron and Cally were heading to the Midwest once they finished ministry school. I knew God was calling them to our church. They came, and have been a tremendous blessing to us.

Aaron and Cally lead our Elevate U School of Supernatural Ministry. They are committed to raising up radical revivalists, lovers of God who are sold out to the vision of impacting and changing culture around them. Part of this vision is to identify the gift, calling, and anointing on a person's life so they can walk out their God-given assignments. I am convinced that a major part of their unique ministry assignment is to partner with God in locating, highlighting, and empowering people who possess the seer anointing.

The Church at large has such a valuable weapon at its disposal, yet it is so rarely talked about. Many of those who operate in this gift have been ignored at best and shunned from congregations at worst. That is why this book is a game changer for those hungry to understand it and grow in it. It's for pastors, leaders, business people, and government officials. It's for everyone, as I believe the seer anointing is essential to the next move of God.

I am huge fan of the unique ways God is moving today in outreach strategies, equipping conferences, and community impact projects. But like everything else God uses to build His kingdom,

He has a strategic purpose in what He is doing and wants to do with the seer anointing. Not just in the corporate church setting, but in board rooms, helping government and law enforcement agencies, or at home in our daily family lives. How in the world can you envision that you might ask? Go ahead and read this book for yourself!

I encourage you, with open hearts and minds, to embrace this composition. It is biblically-based and bathed in Aaron's own personal experience for practical teaching and equipping. My prayer is that the Church will embrace this authentic gift of the Holy Spirit, so that religious filters collapse under the weight of God's glory and the name of Jesus Christ is exalted throughout the earth. Of the increase of His peace and His government, there will be no end!

We love you!

Pastor Ryan Kibbe
Elevation Church
Green Bay, Wisconsin

INTRODUCTION

O f my many experiences, there is one that always stands out as a turning point. I wouldn't discover the significance, the plan as it were, until much later in life. I recall that I was old enough to bathe by myself, but not so old that I didn't require supervision. That's why the door to the bathroom was opened.

As I played with the bubbles and floating toys in the bathtub, movement caught my attention from the corner of my eye. (When things were this vivid, it was always from the corner at first.) There she was. A stunningly beautiful woman, wearing a long and flowing white dress. She walked through the full frame of my vision, left to right, passing by the bathroom door. I cried out, feeling a little exposed at the prospect of a stranger wandering through our home, and even a little embarrassed at the thought that she'd find me naked in the bath. I remember the look of shock on my mother's face when she answered my call for help. There was no visitor.

CHAPTER 1

———

A SEER FROM BIRTH

My story is not that uncommon, except for the fact that I have been a seer for as long as I can remember. I've got some clues as to when the whole thing began, with some supernatural experiences my mother had with 6-month-old me nearby. The important thing is, this gift was always present.

Most seers are either born seers or step into the gift around the time of their salvation or baptism in the Holy Spirit. There are many cases of people receiving the gift after these markers. Praise God; it's getting more and more common!

Some of my earliest memories involve seeing into the spirit or hearing the audible voice of God call my name, which is still a regular part of my experience today. I remember hearing a great leader in the faith, who I view as a spiritual father to this day, talk about the two or three occasions in his lifetime that he'd heard the audible voice of God.

This floored me! I had heard the audible voice of God three times that week, and it was only Wednesday! I didn't quite have an understanding of why I have such a grace to see and hear on my life until recently, when I was talking with a few friends from the International

House of Prayer in Kansas City. As I was sharing my story, one of these friends felt strongly that Psalm 27:10 had something to do with what I had experienced. This verse reads, "For my father and my mother have forsaken me, but the Lord will take me in."

I grew up in a single parent household. This isn't rare in our culture today, but it certainly made for an interesting upbringing. My first real revelation of who God is came in the form of the father I'd never really had.

God had taken up my case in my youth, gifted me incredibly, and placed His protection around me. He took me in, because there was no one around to teach me what was happening to me, or why it was happening. I remember waking up terrified one night, having just dreamed of a monster chasing me through a dark, wooded area, only to find the creature waiting for me on the other side of my sleep, staring at me from the foot of my bed.

Why are young seers usually attacked in manners such as this? I believe it has to do with the enemy seeing the gift and wanting to stifle it as much as possible. We are in a season where the supernatural is drawing more and more people to Christianity, but the Church hasn't done a good job when the mystics come rolling in looking for a place to belong. I believe most mediums and spiritualists are frauds, but a small percentage are seers who were never embraced by the religious system.

Today, a secular view of the afterlife is gaining momentum, in which the ghosts of dead relatives reach out to the living. The very notion calls the Judeo-Christian worldview into question. Even worse, non-discerning seers reinforce this idea by taking each and every supernatural experience at face value (even those that fly in the face of core Christian beliefs).

I say this because, before my salvation, the spiritual world was a very grey area. There were things that were obviously angels and obviously demons, but there was also a world of wild cards I didn't understand. If not for a "feeler gift" I probably would have become one of those people offering free readings on your first phone call.

The enemy also had quite the bullseye on me. I remember waking up with bruises, scratches, and all the things you'd expect from a blockbuster horror movie. I was also terrified of the dark, and developed a terrible fear of alien abduction (of all things) at a young age.

It wasn't until recent years that I began piecing together ancient accounts of fairy abduction, alien abduction, and demonic possession as carrying a common thread. I would physically see things, such as aliens, waiting in the dark. It's no surprise to me now that supernatural people outside of community are claiming to have conversations with aliens. Demons are liars, and it's easy to manipulate a person who is outside of relationship with God.

I also vividly remember the times my gift came in handy, long before I understood it or knew how to use it to its full effect. My grandfather used to call me "eagle eye" because I could always find things that were missing and always had a knack for spotting things before others noticed. Even at an early age, I was using my seer gift. It had very little to do with visual acuity, though my eyes are quite keen. In any situation, I would just watch and wait for an area to stand out. That is where I would look, and the vast majority of the time I would find the missing object in that area. It didn't seem remarkable at the time, but in reality, it was the developing stages of the gift God had given me.

Growing up, I was marked with the heart of an outdoorsman. Fishing, archery—you name it, I was interested. In every situation, whether it was looking for snakes and turtles at the local pond or fishing on Lake Michigan, the gift was being honed further still. God would always highlight just the place where my goal was hiding. I learned to call it luck or favor, but it was more than that. I was using the gifts God had given me to my advantage!

I got saved in a mainline evangelical church, where no one had the language or the knowledge to pastor a young Christian who happened to be a seer. My salvation experience was a prophetic journey to the third heaven and a conversation with Jesus. All at once, I left the room full of teenagers and was in an unfamiliar and wonderful place. Jesus stood before me, shining with a light that seemed to hold every color in frightful harmony. As I fell to the ground, He embraced me. With His touch, something like sand and dust was blown off of my body. I knew it to be sin and shame, gone in an instant. This electric energy plowed through my being, filling me with a holy fear. He then spoke in words filled with love and authority that have marked my journey and continue to form the bedrock of my ministry.

From this moment on I was a radical—a fanatic for this God-man who I had met on a heavenly journey. I'm certain that my leaders either didn't know what to do with me, or simply ignored it and hoped that I would move on to a different church.

In this season of my life, I experienced more of God than I can share within the pages of this book. It was constant revelation, constant ministry, and I saw many people come to Christ. I also experienced more opposition than ever before. There were no longer any grey areas, and the devil wanted to crush what God was doing in and through me. I would come home from a late night of ministry, usually deliverance, home clearing, and evangelism, and see grotesque demonic manifestations standing in my driveway, in the light cast from my headlights. Even remembering them makes the hair on the back of my neck stand up.

On one occasion, I was in fervent prayer for a friend who was suffering from a profound spiritual attack. Suddenly, there was an oppressive presence right behind me. It felt like a person was standing behind me, waiting for an opportunity to attack. With my eyes still closed, I cried out, "In Jesus' name, go!" The presence went over my back and through the wall next to me into a linen closet. All of the boxes on the wall facing me were knocked down. It caused enough commotion for my mother to come into the room and ask what the heck was going on. I've still not told her what it was to this day.

Fresh out of high school my wife, Cally, and I had a supernatural experience that led us to plant a church in our hometown of Kewaunee, Wisconsin. Teenagers running a church! It was crazy, in the best way possible.

I was at a local music festival when I felt God calling me away, into the midst of a deserted tent village. While walking and talking with Him, I was shown a vision of fellow youth in our community who had died from drunk driving accidents, overdoses, and suicides. At the same time, in a different place, my wife was being reminded of a word she had received about planting a church in our community. When we shared the experiences, it became clear that we were to, against all logic, plant a church in the small town of Kewaunee.

We gathered in a friend's living room and chased after a simple Gospel. Before long we moved to a bigger space and saw God do even more outlandish things. Healing, gold dust showing up in strange places, and other miraculous manifestations were a norm and we had no idea what was going on. It was a great relief to learn of Bethel Church in Redding, California. The things we were seeing weren't just happening to us!

After ten years of ministry, we closed the doors of our little church in Kewaunee and moved on to attend the Bethel School of Supernatural Ministry (BSSM) in Redding. Though God had been a constant source of revelation, encouragement, miracles, and transformation, we were tired and burned out. In addition to pastoring, I had been working a job in the disaster relief field. In a rapid season of change, that job came to an end and it became crystal clear that we were to change the way we were doing ministry. Less than a week after my position was terminated (which meant a loss of the only sustaining income we had), my family and I sat at the dinner table in the home of one of the relief organization board member, hearing about a dream he'd had about our family.

"God said I'm supposed to send you to Bethel. I'll double your salary for a year to help afford the added cost of living in California. When can you leave?" The rest is history.

It's my belief that most gifts are passed on through family lines. After attending the Bethel School of Supernatural Ministry, I started opening up to family members about my experiences. Mostly because I wanted to see if any of my family members shared this gift. My mother was quiet on the phone the first time I told her. When she spoke, she told me that she used to see things her mother could not, but it scared my grandmother so she stopped sharing these things and eventually stopped seeing them altogether.

The good will always outweigh the darkness. I've seen heaven more times than I can count. I've had open visions that led to people being healed of all manners of disease, from headaches to cancer. We've even seen the dead raised. When it comes to operating in the seer anointing effectively, I always go back to an exchange I had with Cally years ago.

She looked up at me one day, out of the blue, and said, "I figured it out. You're not really good at everything."

I nodded, slowly.

"You're incredibly blessed with the ability to communicate, so you just figure out how to use that gift and apply it to every problem that comes up. That way, you seem like you can do anything!"

That's exactly it. If you're a seer, figure out how to use this gift to an advantage any time an issue arises. The gifts aren't just for entertainment purposes. They're for winning a spiritual war that shapes this physical world. If we understand this, it's only logical that we would work to create a culture and environment where every weapon at our disposal can be effectively deployed. The Body of Christ is chock full of gifts that function in an offensive role to push back darkness and set the captives free. This is the purpose of the seer anointing. It's not just for your personal benefit, but for building up the Church.

THE SEER ANOINTING

We are in the midst of a season of restoration the likes of which the Church has never seen. With a fresh revelation of the five-fold ministry model (apostles, prophets, teachers, pastors, and evangelists) the Bride of Christ is looking more and more ready for the return of her Bridegroom. This season seems to have a great deal to do with reclaiming the lost pieces of our heritage. As we advance further and further into this swirl of spiritual gifts, we come face to face with a strange fact: One of the most ancient practices we see throughout the Old Testament still goes largely unrestored. That is the seer anointing.

A number of factors contribute to this, but the most prominent of reasons probably lies in the fact that the mystical realm is still an uncomfortable place for many believers. The Church has, on a very large scale, believed the lie that experience is not a trustworthy or valuable piece of our faith walk. Cutting out this key component has left a small but vital slice of our population adrift without a safe place to exercise, experiment, and grow in their gifts. There are even some in the charismatic stream who would make the claim that the seer anointing doesn't exist, or that it should be lumped in with general prophetic gifts. This is a mistake. Our tendency is to downplay the gift we don't understand and lump them in with a more familiar gift. Perhaps we would do better to allow full expression of the gifts, bless what God is doing, and keep an eye on the fruit being produced rather than placing our focus on the things that seem more main-stream and manageable.

There is a difference between the seer anointing and the gift of prophecy. The seer is a part of an experiential root, even more-so than the prophet. They will often experience things in the Kingdom before they read about them or find explanation in study. The "ah-ha" moment for the seer is often one of finding explanation of a part of their rich history and experience in the Scriptures or Christian history.

I would say that the gift of prophecy and the seer anointing are streams which run parallel to one another, or perhaps even different currents in the same prophetic stream. Seers are generally very prophetic, but their experience has a tendency to go beyond what we'd expect from other prophetic gifts. To the seer, Scripture is a playground of visions and encounters. The spiritual realm is real to the seer, not just because they've been told that it is real, but because the seer has firsthand knowledge of how this mysterious dimension works.

Jenn, a friend of mine, is a seer. She has walked in this anointing for a short time, and I had the privilege of discipling her through a good deal of the beginning stages of this process. For Jenn, the seer anointing manifests in her seeing things like flashes of light and color, smoke, and other visual cues. Her desire is to see in full form, and I believe that she'll arrive at this place if she hasn't already by the time this book is published. She has learned to discern the things she has seen, and, more importantly, the purpose of her seeing them.

On a trip to Israel, I watched as Jenn stepped out in a moment of evangelistic risk with a group of strangers. You see, she'd seen flashes of light above them. Through her process, she'd come to the con-clusion that this particular manifestation usually meant an angelic presence. The approach to this particular group ended with at least two miraculous healings and an amazing testimony of releasing the love of Jesus by using the gift she carried as a door to ministry. The gift is immensely useful, desirable, and even fun!

Seers are all around us. Even though I'd place the percentage in the "astonishingly rare" category (I would estimate less than 1% of the general population), there are probably a few in the church you currently attend. You may even walk in this anointing yourself without realizing it. Through a supernatural chain of events, I had the opportunity to attend a very well-known ministry school in California. Even in this group of revivalists, I was hard-pressed to find ten in a class of over one thousand. Still, they were there. I don't think the reason for these low numbers is because the Holy Spirit decided to "slow the flow" with this particular gift. It is far more likely that we, as a Body, simply don't hunger for the seer anointing, so the opportunity for impartation is low. Simply put, if we don't create space for specific gifts of the Spirit to function, we probably will not see them take place. If we automatically become suspicious when we hear of people who claim to possess spiritual gifts, we will see them dwindle even more.

How wonderful it is to see this mindset changing within many different streams of the Church. There is becoming a greater hunger for spiritual gifts, a deeper desire to move away from nominal Christianity and embrace the fullness of the Spirit. For this reason, those who walk in the seer anointing must rise up so they might minister to the rest of the Church.

CHAPTER 2

WHAT IS THE SEER ANOINTING?

The seer anointing causes a great deal of confusion in many circles. Perhaps the most frustrating part is the Bible only references it a few times. The first mention of the actual term "seer" is applied to Samuel in 1 Samuel 9:9. This verse refers to a prophet and a seer as being one in the same. However, there are later references that reflect a deepening understanding of the differences between a seer and a prophet. Among these is 2 Kings 17:13, which reveals a clear differentiation: *Yet the Lord warned Israel and Judah through all His prophets and every seer...* If seers and prophets are the same, this verse makes no sense. We can reasonably conclude that the people of God have grown in their understanding from 1 Samuel 9:9, coming to understand the distinctions between these two gifts. 2 Chronicles 29:25 also tells us that King David had a prophet (Nathan) and a seer (Gad) in his court. This would be a strange designation to make if they are the same thing.

Perhaps the most telling reference is found in Isaiah 30:10, which states, *"Who say to the seers, 'you must not see visions'; and to the prophets, 'You must not prophesy to us what is right'".* This leads to the idea that the seer is prophetically gifted, but tends at the most basic level toward visual processing.

There are a few instances of the seer anointing in the New Testament, but they aren't obvious at first glance. Mark 16:19 is an interesting verse to ponder. *So then, when the Lord had spoken to them, He was received up into heaven and sat down at the right hand of God.* The disciples witnessed this. It wasn't a vision, nor was it a dream. They saw, with their physical eyes, an interaction between the first and third heavens! At the least, this is miraculous, and I believe it gives us a glimpse into how the seer anointing operates.

Another noteworthy passage is the stoning of Stephen in Acts 7. After a long and intricate defense, Stephen (the first martyr in Church history) shifts his dialogue to what He is seeing in the spiritual realm. *But being full of the Holy Spirit, he gazed intently into heaven and saw the glory of God, and Jesus standing at the right hand of God; and he said, "Behold, I see the heavens opened up and the Son of Man standing at the right hand of God"* (Acts 7:55-56). Again, there is nothing to indicate that Stephen was having a vision. He was likely seeing into the third heaven. I can't help but wonder if this was a one-time event, or if he walked in the seer anointing on a regular basis.

Visual processing will be a hallmark of the Kingdom experience of every seer. This is simply a fancy way of saying that God speaks to the seer through their eyes. This means open visions, closed visions, trances, immersive visions, and witnessing activity in the spiritual realm. I do not mean seeing with spiritual eyes. This understanding has left many people with the misconception that they are walking in the seer anointing when they're really just having a prophetic experience that leans toward closed visions or pictures. This is an amazing gift, and it is not to be downplayed. Remember, there is no hierarchy of the gifts. We are all parts of the same body, and every part is unique and valuable (1 Corinthians 12:12-27). It is also possible to have your imagination running while your eyes are open, but this should not be mistaken for the seer anointing. Think of it as the same river, but a different current within the river. If this describes you but you desire to walk in the seer anointing, do not grow discouraged. I have seen quite a few people step into the seer anointing from a place of seeing with spiritual eyes.

I say "visual processing" because many of these manifestations actually use one's physical eyes to receive and interpret the supernatural. The topic never really came to mind until my glasses decided they'd had enough of this life and went to be with Jesus. My prescription isn't so strong that I cannot function day to day without them, though it's a hassle feeling like the world went from crisp, high-definition to grainy, standard def. I opted to go without corrective lenses for a week while my replacement glasses were being made. During this time, I discovered something intriguing: the open visions I was seeing were just as grainy as the rest of the world around me, as were the things I was seeing in the spiritual realm. This settled the question, once and for all: seers see through their physical eyes.

The exact way one sees will be different from one person to another. However, the vividness of the sight varies a great deal for me. Sometimes, it almost looks like double vision, like there are rough forms or an overlay over the scene before me. With focus, these forms will usually become clearer. Other times, it takes some discernment to know if I'm seeing something that is in the physical or the spiritual realm. I think this depends on the situation and the manifestation more than anything else.

In the book of 2 Kings, Elisha not only outs himself as a seer, but also provides strong evidence for impartation of the seer anointing. 2 Kings 6:17 reads, *Then Elisha prayed and said, "O Lord, I pray, open his eyes that he might see." And the Lord opened the servant's eyes and he saw; and behold, the mountain was full of horses and chariots of fire all around Elisha.* Gehazi (Elisha's servant) did not simply share in the vision Elisha was having. There is nothing in the language or context to suggest this. Elisha and Gehazi were both seeing with physical eyes the spiritual realm and the angelic protection of God. The name "Gehazi" even means *valley of vision*.

Seers are not super spiritual individuals, nor are they guaranteed to be trustworthy. Some of the most marvelously anointed people of our time have fallen because of lack of the influence of spiritual mothers and fathers and the healthy boundaries of community. Gehazi was probably a seer from the moment Elisha prayed for him, in spite of the fact that he'd fallen into a great deal of greed and avarice in an earlier escapade (2 Kings 5:20-27).

Some may ask if seers can also be prophets. The answer is a resounding "yes." David's seer, Gad, is also referred to as a prophet in 2 Samuel 24:11. Seers can be anything in the Kingdom. Apparently, they can also be great worship leaders, as evidenced by 2 Chronicles 29:30 and my own personal experience working alongside a young man who functioned in both gifts. He told me he would see angels participating in worship during church services and even heard them join in song with the congregation. That's what I call worship! When heaven decides to join in, it's a good day.

Whatever your gifting happens to be, God wants to use you. If you are a seer and feel called to pastor, then pastor. Whatever your calling, use the combination of your gifts and your personality to advance the Kingdom. If that means an open vision about investing in a certain stock, run with it. God wants you to use the gifts He has given you. Don't leave them wrapped up and hidden!

VISUAL PROCESSING

Though there are many, many, different expressions of the prophetic, I believe there are some that come more naturally and are far more common for the seer. These are (surprise, surprise) linked to *visual processing*. The ones I've observed and experienced thus far are visual cues, closed visions, open visions, immersive visions, trances, spiritual travel, and spiritual sight. As we move forward and experience more and more of Jesus, I have no doubt that this list will fail to be exhaustive, and I hope it isn't. If we haven't gone deeper in the Lord, we've missed glory to glory (2 Corinthians 3:18). That said, we have a need to put language to these things. People are spending far too much time believing they are crazy, broken, or deluded, when they are in fact walking out an exceptional gift.

It is also a mistake to think that a seer cannot flow in other gifts. I've known many seers who were also able to feel the atmosphere, sense the emotions of other people, and move in other prophetic and ministerial gifts. Even though the seer will tend toward visual processing, it shouldn't be seen as a limitation, but rather as another tool in the supernatural box. Furthermore, the combination of gifts in an individual that work in tandem create a "flavor" of personal ministry that is beautiful and unique. Adding the seer anointing to any combination of spiritual gifts will make for even more effective ministry!

Another thing that seers will likely tend toward is a strong sense of communion with nature. I realize this may sound strange, but every seer who I've had the chance to connect with has echoed a similar sentiment; they have all loved to be outside and immersed in God's creation. For me, it almost seems like taking some time away refreshes my gifting. Simply spending time surrounded by the beauty of creation seems to open a door to new insight and a sense of wonder.

I must also give a word of caution regarding visual processing. I have noticed that the enemy tends to attack seers visually. I have been led into what felt like closed visions that follow the flow of a negative emotion. For example, if I was feeling angry in a situation I would see myself standing up and starting a fight (which I sometimes did in my youth). It was as though the enemy was using my awareness of the spiritual realm to seed a vivid idea into my mind that was not from God.

What we consume with our eyes can also have strange effects, some of them not good. For example, Cally and I once watched a video montage entitled something along the lines of *Top Ten Unexplained Events* a few minutes before bed. Most of them were more lame than sinister, but one really shook me up. It was a surveillance video of a woman rocking back and forth in an elevator. As I watched the video I saw a demon, and fear began to creep over me. Clearly this spirit of fear was not from God! (2 Timothy 1:7) Cally and I prayed briefly and then headed off to bed. As Cally got changed, I was alone in our room when the same demon from the video appeared before me. This thing obviously didn't realize whom it was messing with. The Kingdom always wins. Always. However, it still pays to be strategic. Don't watch scary stuff before bed, especially if you're a seer. You don't want to walk into fights with the enemy unless you are called there. This doesn't mean you run when the devil tries to bring hell to your doorstep, just don't go looking for it!

All of the gifts are forms of communication God chooses. We don't get to choose how He reveals Himself to us, but we can initiate conversation with Him. We are His children, after all.

The remainder of this chapter includes quick, practical descriptions of each expression of the prophetic and the seer anointing. I've also included an activation for each section, which I invite you to take the time and risk to pursue. Stretching these areas of your walk with God can and will bear fruit if you simply let God perform His work in you!

VISUAL CUES

Visual cues aren't visions, they are more like a Holy Spirit highlight on something that would normally be mundane in context. God will sometimes highlight a person's hair or eye color, a specific article of clothing, or even things physically located around an individual as a clue that leads to the prophetic message He wants to leave them with. The fullness of the experience won't usually be constrained within a red shirt someone is wearing; the Holy Spirit simply uses this as an entry point to lead a seer on a prophetic journey toward an encounter that begins with a visual clue.

I once had a supernatural opportunity to encourage someone, which began with God highlighting her simply because of the clothing she was wearing. The only thing I had to go on was the fact that there was something about her attire that drew me toward her. The end result was more than one incredibly accurate word of knowledge and a message from God that shook her to her very core (in a good way).

If it helps, think of these sorts of cues in the same way that a feeler might just "know," deep in their emotions, that God has chosen a particular person to receive ministry. God highlights the people who are in the crosshairs of a love encounter, and He does it in the way we will most easily understand. To say that God is whispering in a "still small voice" isn't entirely accurate. It's more like He is reaching out, but we don't understand His voice. Every account of God speaking in the New Testament is loud enough for large groups to hear, but we are sometimes convinced that we need to listen better because He is intentionally making it hard for us to hear Him. God does not toy with His children! It seems He speaks clearly more often than we are comfortable to admit.

While participating in a mock disaster training with Crisis Response International awhile back, my team was tasked with responding to an airplane crash in a wooded area. We had already spent a few days together building trust, and the briefing on our mission was very simple: a plane had gone down (they did a great job of making it realistic!) and a number of survivors were missing, though some had gathered near the wreckage of the fuselage. As our transport entered the scene, I sensed God highlight a particular part of the woods. I turned to the rest of the team and told them, "I know where one of the survivors is. Over there, in the woods." Assignments were handed out and we began the search and rescue mission. Within five minutes, we had the survivor on a backboard and were headed to the mobile triage tent. It's hard to describe why that part of the woods looked different for a split second, but something inside of me just knew there was a person in that area. This aspect of the seer anointing is often just that—a knowing. Other times, it looks like a ripple of color or light, and there are times when it is almost like an outline around a certain place, person, or object that captures the attention of the seer. Regardless, it is a common way that God communicates with visual processors.

Another visual cue that is common among seers is a sense of *déjà vu,* or even seeing a person and having the strong impression that you have seen them before even though you have not. This happens more often than we probably notice. It is not limited to the seer anointing, though I do think it happens more often among seers. I think it is along the lines of picking up on a familiar anointing, gift, or even seeing a call on someone's life that mirrors a person you already know.

I have personally begun taking risks in this area. When I see someone who just seems to remind me of another person, I'll take that as an open door to prophecy over that person. I typically start out by speaking out things I know about the character of the person they remind me of. The vast majority of the time, it's spot on! The thing I picked up on isn't a body feature or a similar haircut, it's a similarity between the person's spirit and that of the person I already know!

Activation: The next time you're in a setting in which you can comfortably practice your gifting (or while you are out shopping, depending on how much you desire to risk), attempt to initiate an encounter by asking the Holy Spirit to highlight something about a person you can see with your physical eyes. God often uses clothing or physical attributes to move to a deeper level, so don't be afraid of the obvious. Remember, this isn't about getting it right 100% of the time, it's about taking a risk and learning to speak another language of the prophetic realm.

Try seeking visual cues next time you or a loved one loses something. Ask God to take you on an adventure and use your eyes to follow the trail He creates for you.

CLOSED VISIONS

Closed visions take place in the confines of your mind. Sometimes they are pictures, words, or even what adds up to a short movie playing in your imagination. The truth of the matter is they are common manifestations that don't always feel holy and inspired. More often than not it feels as though your mind is wandering, but in these moments the key is risk and experimentation. Simply put, Jesus talks to some people—seers in particular—in pictures and visuals. I imagine many let prophetic opportunities slip by because they fail to see the value of these visuals in the moment. When you see something in your mind's eye, share it and see if it resonates with the person in front of you. What I've begun experimenting with is holding onto these visuals for later. If I see something in my mind while worshiping, I will write it down as soon as I can and ask the Holy Spirit if it's for someone in the room. More often than not, He'll highlight the person who He wants to bless through the vision.

On one occasion, I was doing a prophetic activation where we were literally blindfolded and asked to speak a prophetic word over a randomized person placed in front of us. I hated activations like this one, as they usually raised my stress levels and I had a difficult time hearing God clearly in the past when the pressure was on. For some reason, I didn't feel any pressure on this occasion as I asked God for a word. All that came to mind was a cheetah, an image of which briefly popped into my head. I shared what I saw, then sort of groped around for a bit looking for some sort of interpretation. What God had shown me was enough. The girl in front of me had been given a stuffed cheetah in grade school and the nickname, "cheetah" had followed her for most of her school days. Clearly this was an accurate word from the Lord!

For some reason, music seems to be a great way to grease the wheels of this prophetic expression. I don't know why, but most of the people I've encountered would report that it was easier to see a closed vision when they were listening to music. I remember very clearly doing this in the car as a young man. I'd sit in the back seat while my mother drove and listen to my music through headphones. All the while, it was like I was watching movies in my head. Looking back, I realize these were closed visions of the spiritual state of the world around me. I had no idea at the time!

Visions in general can be a very practical form of communication with God. On one occasion, my wife and I were wrapping up a night of ministry with some friends in central Illinois when a practical issue came up. My buddy, Craig, had lost his keys. As seven people searched for them with no luck, I decided it wouldn't hurt to tap into the seer anointing to aid in the search. I closed my eyes and immediately saw a picture of Craig's guitar case. I told the person who was searching for the keys with me and we approached Craig. I told him he needed to check his guitar case, and the missing keys were recovered moments later. This gift isn't just for high and lofty things, but is useful for everyday life!

Activation: Put on some worship music and allow your mind to wander but watch for a shift in your thoughts. Typically, you will begin to "see" things in your mind that are not a part of your normal mental routine. (For example, you may see citrus trees when you live in the Midwest.) Write down, record, or commit to memory what you see. The next time you're around a group of people, ask God to show you the person this picture was for. This would work perfectly before attending a worship service, as most people who show up at church are hungry to hear from God.

OPEN VISIONS

There are a few different streams of thought regarding *open visions* floating around the Church today, but the one that is probably the most common is described as seeing the content of a closed vision, but with your eyes open. In other words, you physically see something. Some describe it as seeing the image like it's being projected on a particular surface, or like a giant television screen has appeared over the subject of the vision while the vision itself plays out.

The frequency of this type of vision will vary greatly from one person to another, but it is not a matter of open visions being superior to any other experience. Several years ago, I met a woman who would go into virtually any social setting and see what looked like a chalkboard over the head of every person in the room. She'd see words written on each chalkboard that told some detail of the person's life. These ranged from prayer needs, to unused gifts, to sin habits that had not been rooted out. These insights allowed her to minister in power to almost anyone she encountered. Many others can count on one hand the number of open visions they have experienced. Honestly, whenever I hear someone say something to the effect of, "I've only had two visions in my life, so when they happen I pay attention" it breaks my heart a little. It comes across a bit like a spiritual poverty mindset. "God will only encounter me in a supernatural way if it's about something really, really important" seems to be the belief. I've seen an open vision when asking God where I left my car keys. This isn't about elitism or about placing different value on different experiences. God is infinite, so our experiences of Him should be also.

There is, however, an element of God's sovereignty in the occurrence and frequency of open visions. That said, I think we can positions ourselves to see them more often. Priming the pump looks like practicing using our imagination with our eyes open instead of shut. The same experience of a closed vision can be had with the eyes opened. Personally, I've seen the frequency of open visions in my life increase as I've made the effort to lean into God's presence without closing my eyes.

An interesting observation I have made over the years is open visions seem to stick with you. I've had hundreds, maybe thousands, of closed visions and there aren't very many that I can remember off the top of my head. Though I have not had nearly as many open visions, I can remember each and every one of them in vivid detail. There is something about the process of seeing with your physical eyes that causes a vision to stay with you, and sharing it openly makes it even harder to forget.

Activation: Try it out. The next time you have the opportunity to minister to someone, attempt to access your redeemed imagination while your eyes are open. This may not work the first time you attempt it, but I encourage you to continue trying. Allow your mind to be the canvas that Jesus can create His masterpiece on.

IMMERSIVE VISIONS

Immersive visions are one of the hallmarks of the seer anointing. They go beyond open visions into a realm that is almost hard to explain and near impossible to activate (though if you're looking for an activation, I'd expect an increase in the same manner as open visions). In an immersive vision, it actually looks like there is an object, animal, or person in the room with you that isn't physically there. Sometimes these are plain as day and require little discerning; other times, a great deal of interpretation is needed. On one occasion, I saw a man in a suit standing behind a friend of mine with his hands on my friend's shoulders, his head bowed in prayer. I wondered if a new intern had been taken on, as I didn't recognize the fellow at all. When I looked back, the man in the suit was gone. I shared this vision with my friend, then grabbed my phone and did a little searching. Within a few minutes I received a word from God and came upon a picture of the man I'd seen. It was John G. Lake. Now, do I believe I'd seen a long-dead revivalist laying hands on my friend in the literal, God sent the spirit of John G. Lake to pray for my friend, sense? Maybe. But it's far more likely that God was showing me that my friend was either receiving a mantle or walking in a similar anointing as John G. Lake.

On another occasion, my wife and I were ministering in the home of a woman who had simply lost her fire for life when I saw a house cat the size of a medium dog walk across the room from left to right, directly in front of me. I was a bit shocked, and jumped slightly. The cat crouched down, then sprang and pounced on a small black fox and carried it out of the room, the way that a tabby cat would carry off a mouse. Song of Solomon 2:15 immediately jumped into my mind. "Catch the foxes for us, the little foxes that are ruining the vineyards…". This gave me a solid strategy for how to pray for this woman and her situation. It wasn't necessarily the major things that were stealing her joy, numerous as they were. It was the little foxes; the grating daily struggles that were wearing her down and stealing her victory.

These kinds of visions will often require interpretation. I know a seer from Canada named Jessica who sees many immersive visions of animals. Part of her journey has been to sort out what specific animals tend to mean, and how she can partner with God when He reveals these sorts of things to her. It isn't that God has hidden things from her; He is inviting her on an intimate journey of discovering what the things He is showing her mean!

Bill Johnson often quotes Proverbs 25:2, "It is the glory of God to conceal a matter, but the glory of kings is to search out a matter," or, as he puts it, "When God hides something from you, it's because He is inviting you into your royal identity."

Though seeing animals in the spiritual realm was not a new manifestation for her, she began to see recurring themes. One of them was seeing dogs around her with great regularity. She'd come to the conclusion that dogs were probably demonic, but this meant a lot of what she was seeing was demonic. After a bit of probing I discovered, in the physical realm, she associated dogs with comfort, safety, and love. Before long, she realized seeing dogs meant, for her, that angels were near and active! This leads to another point: Be wary of any method of interpretation which takes a shortcut around the Holy Spirit. For example; if you were to have a dream or vision about a snake, what would you think? For most people, the answer is going to be lying, venom, double speak, and a whole world of fear and negativity. For me, most of the time when I see a snake it's tied to healing (Numbers 21:9) and regeneration (the Celtic Christians believed that a snake shedding its skin was symbolic of salvation; the old self dying and the new coming into being). This probably has to do with the fact that I am a lover of reptiles, idolizing Steve Irwin as a child.

God speaks to you through your experience and personality. He created you with desires, dreams, tastes, and drives. He won't circumvent who you are, but rather He will use every bit of who you are—your redeemed self—to advance the Kingdom.

TRANCES

There seems to be a stigma around *trances*, maybe more than any other expression of the prophetic realm. This has much to do with an unhealthy association between trances and the new age movement. In reality, trances appear many times in the Scripture, and I would argue that if we look at the experiences described by prophets in the Old and New Testaments, we would see trances as one of the most common manifestations of the gift of prophecy.

The key feature of a trance is the one experiencing it has no cognizance while the trance is happening. The trance drowns out all stimuli going on around the person. Their body may be laying on the floor or sitting in a chair, but their consciousness is doing something completely different and removed from the environment. They may be meeting a lost loved one in heaven, having an all-encompassing vision of the future, or having a conversation with Jesus on His throne (accounts of all of these exist, and I've experienced many of them myself).

The Scriptures are marked with trances. In Acts 10:9-16, Peter falls into a trance and the end result is the reversal of the whole Jewish dietary system for believers who are in Christ! In Acts 22:17, Paul is actually warned to flee from the region of Judea in—you guessed it—a trance. That experience saved Paul's life! The book of Revelation contains rich prophetic and apocalyptic experiences that John the Revelator likely received while in a trance state. These are manifestations that simply cannot be ignored.

Trances are deeply tied to the will and move of the Holy Spirit, but one noteworthy point I can make from my own experience is that intimacy with God is directly correlated to the frequency of trances. I also believe trances can be stirred up (I'll get to this later). Trances have been a very normal and consistent part of my spiritual journey, but they also function as a sort of spiritual thermometer. If I walk through a season without seeing many trances, it is almost always a season in which my spiritual disciplines have tapered off and my prayer life has suffered in favor of getting things done in the physical realm. One feature of trances I have noticed is they are usually either very personal or carry a corporate significance. Some of the richest healing and redemption of my past has come through trances, and many of the corporate words I hear from God come from being in a trance state. I've never received a word for another individual during a trance. This may not be a rule, but it's been a theme I have noticed in my life.

I've spoken to a young prophet named Brendan who has had many trances while driving! The setting isn't important, but behind the wheel might not be the place to press for this particular experience. The saying, "Jesus, take the wheel" gains a whole new meaning here! At the same time, trances aren't anything to fear. They are an opportunity for the Holy Spirit to do marvelous things in the life of the recipient.

Deep emotional healing can happen in the midst of a trance. I had one such encounter while taking a boat ride on the Sea of Galilee. My grandfather had died two years prior. He was the man who raised me, and a father in a very real sense. He was always private about things like religion and toward the end of his life his demeanor had so softened that I often wondered if He had met Jesus. That boat trip began to remind me of growing up on Grandpa's fishing boat and all the time we'd shared together. Before I knew it, I was in a trance. This was unlike any trance I'd experienced before, because I was suddenly sitting across from my grandfather in the old fishing boat. He told me about how he had, in fact, surrendered to God in the last season of his life. He told me about how wonderful things were now, and how he finally understood why I had devoted my life to the cause of the Gospel. It all made sense to him now. Now, I know that some of you are probably thinking, "Doesn't the Bible say you shouldn't try to contact the dead?" Indeed, it does. (See Deuteronomy 18:11.) However, if God in His sovereignty decided to allow such a thing to take place, especially when I did not intend to do it, I'm not going to complain or overthink it. If that's the way God wants to heal the memories of my past, I'm all in!

Have you ever been lost in thought or daydreaming and the world seemed to slip away? I believe trances come from the same "place" of allowing our mind to wander *with* God. It may even be, as we grow in intimacy with God and make intentional time to press into His presence, that trances become more common in our experience.

Activation: Because of the tie to intimacy with God, try pressing into a spiritual discipline. Attempt a fast if the grace is there. Try getting up early a few days a week, or staying up late to read your Bible and pray. If giving up food is too difficult, choosing a day to fast sleep with a night watch can also be very effective. Staying up through the night interceding, praying, and worshipping can be a huge key to breakthrough in the spiritual realm and open doors for these mystical gifts to function. Though all gifts flow from intimacy with and love for God, trances seem especially tied to this place. Wait on the Lord and be honest about your desire to have this experience. Seek a place of deeper intimacy with God and the chances are good that trances will follow.

SPIRITUAL TRAVEL

In the life of the seer it seems that heavenly encounters are more common. Many have reported these sorts of experience, from the Prophet Ezekiel to the Apostle John. The tradition of heavenly experiences continues today. These manifestations have some overlap with trances, but the details of the experience seem different enough that they warrant their own distinction.

The term *spiritual travel* will, no doubt, send up red flags for some readers. Astral projection is a common claim of the New Age, the occult, and many other fringe groups. This is in no way what we are talking about. When you hear the phrase "spiritual travel," the first thing you should realize is this sort of thing must be subjected to the Holy Spirit. That means the seer isn't going to wake up tomorrow morning and think, "I wonder what the weather is like in Tahiti, I think I'll just send my spirit on a quick jaunt to find out!" Most of the time, these experiences are going to look more like Paul's account in 2 Corinthians 12 of a man who was transported to the third heaven.

These experiences most often go along with a trance, but that's not always the case. I remember a time of very intense corporate worship when I was suddenly aware of two realities, running parallel to one another. With my ears, I could hear the worship music, but every other sense was suddenly engulfed with the scene of Revelation 4. I saw and heard the peals of thunder and flashes of lightning. The thrones of the elders, the emerald rainbow, the lamps burning, and everything from that chapter was suddenly happening around me. I was walking amidst the scene in heaven. This went on for several minutes before I was jarringly shocked back into my body. Just then, one of the ministry leaders stepped up to the microphone and said, "I don't know why, but I really feel like we need to read Revelation 4." I nearly fell down! Before this person spoke, I was wondering if I was losing my mind. God is so ridiculously good to confirm what He is doing!

This wasn't the first time God had immediately confirmed what He was showing me and I'm sure it won't be the last. On another occasion, I was caught up in a trance and saw the roof of the building that I was seated in melt away like wax. There, in the sky, a door opened. As I walked through the door, I was suddenly in a large and ornate room. It felt like a staging area for deployment of angels, resources, and, presumably, whatever heaven had in store for earth. The experience that followed had much to do with prophetic seasons and the future of the prophets within the Church. The Apostle Paul had at least one experience like this, though at the time of the writing of 2 Corinthians 12:1-4 it would be hard to imagine this was a normal experience for him.

I don't claim to be greater than the Apostle Paul, but I do know that the promise of "greater things" in John 14 should extend past what the first century Church experienced. We have been building a mystic history for 2000 years! We don't need a restoration of the first century Church, we need a continuation of what has been taking place since the Resurrection! This has been happening in different remnants of the Christian tradition, most notably among the Catholics.

Remember, miracles and mystic experiences don't automatically mean sound doctrine is present. It is a grave mistake to claim that you know God's motive in supernatural experiences. It could be that He is just lovingly interacting with His children. I have many close friends in the Catholic faith who love Jesus in the same radical way that is exhibited by the folks in our movement.

St. Faustina wrote in her diary, "November 27, 1936. Today I was in heaven, in spirit, and I saw its unconceivable beauties and the happiness that awaits us after death. I saw how all creatures give ceaseless praise and glory to God" (Kowalska 2005, 201). This is not aberrant behavior among saints. St. Catherine, Sister Josefa Menendez, and many others claimed these sorts of experience (along with things we would call open visions, closed visions, spiritual sight, etc.). Thank God that we're *all* saints, according to the New Testament! These manifestations aren't only open to the "super-spiritual." Every believer can experience them!

For too long we have placed every promise of heaven in a removed future or a distant past. In the modern era, people are having spiritual encounters at a rate that truly feels like "glory to glory." I don't know why this seems to be on the rise, but if it is truly growing, I'm surprised this acceleration has taken this long to occur. We are the Church, and heaven isn't just our future.

Ephesians 2:4-7 is rich with theology. *But God, being rich in mercy, because of His great love with which He loved us, even when we were dead in our transgressions, made us alive together with Christ (by grace you have been saved), and raised us up with Him, and seated us with Him in the heavenly places in Christ Jesus, so that in the ages to come He might show the surpassing riches of His grace in kindness toward us in Christ Jesus.*

For example, the idea that our Bibles translate the Greek word *aion* as "ages to come" (v. 7), when the word literally means something more like "for your entire lifetime, without ceasing." The most interesting point to ponder is verse 6, "and raised us up with Him, and seated us with Him in the heavenly places in Christ Jesus." So, putting those together, we have been raised up with Jesus and we exist at the same time in heaven and on earth, so that we can live a lifetime of discovering the riches of His grace.

This means we have access to heaven now! It doesn't mean we have to wait until death to start seeing God's goodness, nor do we have to wait until some mythical "end times" to see the Church begin to put on her glory! (Never mind the fact that we are in the end times according to Peter in Acts 2:17.) We are *already* seated in heavenly places. We *already* have unprecedented access to heaven. When I am sitting in my recliner the only thing that stops me from getting a snack from the kitchen is laziness, or my wife telling me we're out of snacks. But what if she's lying? What if she thinks the cabinet is empty but she hasn't checked? This is the mindset the Church has had for far too long. Fear and outright unbiblical teaching has limited the move of the Holy Spirit in the name of "sound doctrine." We must take the risk to taste and see that He is good!

Activation: The experience of spiritual travel is, again, powerfully tied to intimacy and the expectancy of the believer. I think a big part of it has to do with changing one's mindset. When heaven is alive and real and present, it's easier to imagine going there. I remember hearing a story when I was in Israel about a prophetic group that came to do ministry. This group didn't understand fully the importance of being sensitive to different cultures, and, inevitably, the mindset of the American and Israeli churches collided head-on. One of the Israeli men received a word about dying in the next year, or so he thought. The word was about seeing the Kingdom manifest in the coming year, but his paradigm told him that seeing the Kingdom meant physical death.

When we renew our minds to the availability of heaven, we will have the opportunity to access it in *this* life, though not in full. Get hungry, read other people's accounts, and press into the heart of Jesus. Do not read the New Testament with an unattainable view of "the good old days," but see it as a mandate for our glory to glory generation to experience the same things, and even greater things!

SPIRITUAL SIGHT

Now we come to the greatest point of distinction between the seer anointing and other prophetic expressions. Simply put, *spiritual sight* is seeing into the spiritual realm—the second and third heavens. The second heaven represents the realm of angels and demons, while the third heaven is heaven itself in the literal sense. Interpretation is sometimes needed in this realm, but more often than not it is a matter of discerning of spirits. Not every angel is an angel, at least not in the sense that we are used to.

The spiritual realm can be a place of great activity or a place of silence. Most people seem to have the misconception that there is always a flood of activity going on, and that seers are constantly privy to the bustle and rush of spiritual beings carrying out assignments. In reality, only God is omnipresent. It is possible to encounter God at every turn, but the seer will not see angels and demons around every corner. There will be some things that are more commonplace than others—angels that seem to be assigned to the seer or their family, demons that seem to come around more than others, certain manifestations of the Holy Spirit, etc.

When it comes to angels and demons, there is great diversity. Colors, sizes, and even different racial features. The one thing I have not noticed is gender. Even though I've seen angels that appear more feminine or masculine, I've never seen one that looked specifically female. I don't think that this means all angels are male. Rather, it means angels aren't of any gender whatsoever. The argument can be made that Scripture portrays angels as masculine because it often uses masculine language to describe them, but this may have more to do with the time period in which the Scriptures were written, with masculine language being used to signify authority and power than a gender-specific trait that I believe angels do not possess.

The third heaven will provide better information and strategy than the second heaven. Knowing the movement of angels and demons can be helpful and interacting with them is pivotal, but the activity of heaven is the greatest power source for the seer. It is easy to get sidetracked, especially when a season of great spiritual activity is at hand, but remember that Jesus literally has all of the answers. A glimpse of what heaven is doing is more valuable than a clear view of every angelic and demonic strategy. Look for what God is doing and bless that manifestation. If you can partner with it in some way, jump on the opportunity. He never fails.

Another point to consider is the importance of wielding this manifestation well. To be blunt, I mistrust any seer that claims to see into the spiritual realm perpetually. There was a season of my life where this happened, and it was mentally, physically, and spiritually exhausting. This season taught me that the gift can be turned on and off. Mastery of the gift, if there is such a thing, has to involve coming to a place where you can either focus past what you are seeing or control some of the content. To put it another way, I have shared everything I have seen with my wife since we've been together. We began dating in high school and were married young. I have been more open with her than I have been with anyone else in my life. I have told her every story and every experience, and she was present with me for many, many supernatural events.

One day, I felt led by the Spirit to pray an impartation for her, to open her eyes to the spiritual realm the way I saw it. She refused— flatly, even violently. At this stage, much of what I was seeing was demonic (partially because of the sort of ministry we were doing and partially because we were in a particularly difficult season of "plowing" as we pushed back the darkness). She had no desire to tangle with the sort of things I was encountering regularly.

If you recall, the gift of prophecy is subject to the prophet/prophetic person (1 Corinthians 14:32). This gift is no different. I remember asking people if they wanted their eyes opened and their response being something along the lines of, "only if I can't see demons." The reality is we are at war, and the spiritual realm is affected by the battle every day. To cut off an intel stream is a bad plan. That said, I have seen more and more light (rather than darkness) the longer I have walked in this anointing. The more the Kingdom advances, the more we see Jesus and the less we see the enemy and his influences. This is a point of promise. Though attacks come, and they may be more intense early on, it gets so much better. Imagine seeing the cloud of witnesses from Hebrews 12 cheering you on as you endeavor to advance the Kingdom! I have spoken with many seers who have experienced just that.

Another key is tuning the seer anointing to work alongside and in conjunction with other spiritual gifts you may possess. For example, if you are also a feeler (sort of the emotional equivalent of the seer anointing), begin paying attention to what is happening in the spiritual realm when you get an emotional cue. You will eventually reach the point of knowing what sort of spirit you are seeing and dealing with simply by using these two gifts in accord with one another. If you are particularly anointed in the gift of tongues, seeing in the Spirit could also show you what sort of impact that gift has on the unseen realm.

There's just one other manifestation of the seer anointing I want to address here, and that is seeing the human spirit. This has been a fairly recent development for me, but it's worth mentioning. I remember the first time I saw it. My wife and I were walking into a church service when I experienced an almost trance-like flash of insight. For just a few seconds I was walking with a great procession of warriors who were dressed in armor and wielded all sorts of different weapons. It wasn't until I looked around that I realized what had happened. I had glimpsed the spirits of the people entering the service around me.

This has happened on many occasions since. It is almost like seeing a physical manifestation of gifts, anointings, and callings on people. Even the weak points that need shoring up sometimes shine through. It's the best kind of intelligence, the sort that we can use to edify and encourage the Body.

Activation: If you know another seer, start asking them if they are seeing the same things you are, or at least if something is coming up the same area. If you feel you can trust this person, doing this regularly can be a great way to hone your gift. For example, if you normally see abstract things (flashes of light, color, etc.) and know someone that sees in a different way, start asking them questions. *Do you see something there?* This doesn't mean turning off your discernment, but it could be a good communal path to interpreting and growing in your gift.

THE SEER AND DREAMS

I almost hesitate to write about dreams, simply because this area is probably the least limited to those who walk in the seer anointing. As a matter of fact, I have spoken to many people who have prophetic dreams fairly regularly but do not consider themselves to be at all prophetic. It is clear to me that prophetic dreams are available to all believers. However, I have also never met a seer who was *not* a dreamer. For this reason, it is prudent to at least touch on this topic.

Assuming one sleeps an average of eight hours per night (a dream for many, I'm sure), a conservative estimate of the time spent asleep over the course of one year is more than 2,500 hours. This equates to more than 100 full days per year spent asleep! Is this nothing more than wasted time? I don't know about you, but I serve a God who wastes *nothing*.

Seers will dream, and they will most likely dream in vivid color and in amazingly complex allegories. This has to do with a bent toward visual processing more than anything else. Allegorical dreams can lead to breathtaking revelation if they are approached with the guidance of the Holy Spirit. I would hesitate to use interpretation books and guides. The authors are most likely well-meaning people that may have genuine revelation on the interpretation of dreams, but your dreams are probably far too personal to trust to a chart that claims things like "every cat in a dream represents a dead relative." God is not a God of rigid formulas but One who desires intimate relationship with us. We can trust Him to make what He is saying clear.

One of the most profound spiritual experiences of my life was born during a dream and the process of interpreting that dream. I had this dream while taking a course on dream interpretation. It's funny how God does things, isn't it? It was vivid and wild and, in some ways, very personal. At the dream's climax, I was given a brand-new car, which for some reason was parked between a car that I used to own and another old beater that I had never seen before. The important thing was the brand-new car. I knew in the dream that it was mine, but I had never seen one like it before. It was a supercar, like a Ferrari or Lamborghini, but the model was completely foreign to me. Those years of watching *Top Gear* apparently did nothing in this instance!

When I woke I typed the dream up as fast as I could and sent it to some members of my class. This was a dream I just needed to have interpreted! If you have a dream that just seems to "stick with you," write it down or record yourself describing it. (All smartphones have an ability to record memos.) You can then share it with others when appropriate. Bringing it to the larger community of faith can unlock revelation you may never tap into otherwise.

The shocker to me came after I sent the email. Suddenly, I felt strongly compelled to go online and attempt to find the car from my dream. I had never seen a car like it before, so I knew it was a long shot. Much to my surprise, it didn't take long to find the car. Even more surprising, I found that it was a concept car that was more than a year away from being produced.

There is another side to dreams for the seer: they can be a gate through which the enemy attempts to levy spiritual attacks. Many of the seers who I have spent time with have shared their experiences of great difficulties during the night.

When we sleep, we are not "inactive." When you plug your smartphone in to charge for the night, you are not technically "using" it, but this does not mean nothing is happening to it. Power is flowing into it, signals are being sent and received, apps are running in the background, and you will likely receive texts or emails from your friends who don't understand the concept of sleep.

Have you ever woken up feeling spiritually and emotionally exhausted in spite of the fact that you got eight or more hours of uninterrupted sleep? This is not always a sign of spiritual warfare, but sometimes it is. I believe we can interact with the spiritual realm as we dream. Job 4:12-21 recounts a moment when one of Jobs friends, Eliphaz, is visited by an evil spirit in his sleep. The spirit sought to convince Eliphaz to question God's goodness and righteousness.

We also know God can speak to us in our sleep from countless biblical examples from the likes of Jacob (Genesis 20 and 31), Daniel (Daniel 7), Solomon (1 Kings 3), and even Jesus' earthly father, Joseph, in Matthew 1. I don't believe that the enemy has the same access to our sleep, but I do believe he can gain *some* access.

I remember one season in particular where it seemed like every night there was some demonic temptation or battle that would take place in my dreams. There was no fear involved, which seemed strange at the time. It was almost like the fighting was somehow joyous. The end of that season was marked with personal victory for my family and I, and it is my belief that I was fighting and pushing back the forces of darkness while I slept!

The simple act of recognizing that spiritual attacks that come through dreams offer the opportunity to fight back and be victorious can sometimes be all that is needed to break the cycle. Revelation in this area leads to a new outlook on what is taking place. You have the authority to turn the tides any time the enemy attacks. The authority that Jesus holds over the enemy is accessible for His church! According to Mark 16:17, the first sign that will follow believers is the defeat of the enemy (casting out demons). This also applies to dreams and attacks in the night. Your dreams are just another opportunity to see Jesus take back territory that the enemy has stolen.

Seers also tend to walk in the gift of interpretation. I have interpreted dreams for others on many occasions. When these dreams are prophetic in nature, I will almost always "see" the dream playing in my mind as the person is describing it to me. From there, it is simply a matter of listening to the Holy Spirit as He guides you and the dreamer on the journey to understand what God is saying. Start by asking Him to highlight specific things in the dream that He is using to speak to the dreamer. Colors, things that stand out in the setting, smells, or even what people in the dream may represent beyond the norm can all be clues that lead to what God is saying. Remember, dreams are often personal revelation for the dreamer. This makes interpretation books and web searches of questionable value. I believe God sometimes speaks in symbols that are hard to understand to provide an opportunity to lean into the community of believers! It is a chance to connect with other people in the Church and discern what God is saying together.

CHAPTER 3

THIN PLACES

Celtic Christians had a term for places where great spiritual activity occurred. They called them *thin places*. This term has experienced a powerful resurgence in our present day, as Celtic symbols and spirituality have become more popular in our culture. According to the Celtics, thin places are spots where the boundary between the heavens is especially thin. I have experienced a number of thin places and therefore have a hard time *not* believing in them. From worship services where God's presence is tangible to fishing holes deep in the Wisconsin woods, there just seem to be certain spots where the reality of the Kingdom is much easier to experience.

I believe the Old Testament Bethel is such a place. In the familiar story, Jacob stops to rest and has a dream in which he sees a ladder going from the earth to heaven with angels ascending and descending. He even sees God in the dream! When Jacob awakes, he declares "Surely the Lord is in this place, and I did not know it." He even goes on to say, "How awesome is this place! This is none other than the house of God, and this is the gate of heaven" (see Genesis 28:16-17). Jacob just happened to pick a place of unusual supernatural activity as his rest stop!

Some mistakenly assume that every place of great beauty is a thin place. These places may inspire emotion, but that doesn't mean they are spots where God's glory is made manifest. When we talk about thin places, we are talking about places where angels come and go, where the Presence of God is especially and undeniably strong, or where past events have left an indelible impression on the physical realm. I don't think God simply made some places of great beauty to be "holy ground," though it is hard to look on Mt. Shasta in Northern California without a twinge of breathless wonder. (Perhaps thin places are spots in creation where God decided to have a little fun and show off for His children!) Thin places like Bethel in Genesis 28 do naturally exist, waiting for us to stumble upon them. However, I think they are more commonly created. I believe there are three ways this can take place: cultivation, activation, and monuments of breakthrough.

COMMON WAYS THAT THIN PLACES ARE CREATED

Cultivated thin places are probably the most common. A prophetic culture—an environment where prophetic ministry is embraced and encouraged—and anointed worship makes an impact on the atmosphere of a location that simply brings a greater measure of heaven. Friends of mine who are especially sensitive to the spiritual realm will often comment on how a certain church or even a person's home will have a peace in the atmosphere that is almost tangible. I have personally walked into churches and been overwhelmed by the presence of God when nothing was going on; there was no service or meeting taking place but the presence of God lingered in the building in a tangible way. It seems that there is something about pure and authentic worship taking place that has a profound impact on a spiritual atmosphere over a period of time. I'm reminded of the International

House of Prayer in Kansas City, Missouri (IHOP-KC), where prayer and worship has been taking place 24/7/365 for nearly two decades. Literally, a prayer meeting began in 1999 and has never stopped. The atmosphere in that place is thick and rich with the presence of God. They have cultivated a thin place through perpetual service to the Lord and it has become an international attraction.

Activated thin places are different than cultivated ones. Activated places are found where profound events have taken place, almost as though they become thin places instantaneously after key events. The Garden of Gethsemane is one such place.

On a trip to Jerusalem earlier this year I saw many "holy" sites. I say "holy" in quotes because a common joke when one returns from a trip to Israel is to ask, "Did you see all three places where Jesus was buried?" There are rival spots that each compete for the title of the "real place" where Jesus was buried. Of these places, the site that impacted me the most was the Garden of Gethsemane.

Before we entered, we walked past a small, gated garden of olive trees. As we did, I saw something I had never seen before. There were old, gnarly-looking olive trees in the gated area, and in front of every one of them stood a large angel holding a sword out in front of them with the tip pointed down, into the ground. As we entered the cathedral that was erected over the stone where Jesus purportedly travailed before His crucifixion, I saw angels in the spiritual realm approaching the stone and touching it, much like many of the visitors did in the physical realm. This was a strange sight to be sure.

Afterward, our tour guide explained that the olive trees outside were called "the silent witnesses." They were more than 2,000 years old and actually existed when Jesus was alive. Those same trees I saw were in the same spots in this garden on the night Jesus was arrested.

Why would angels accompany these trees? To be fair, I have no idea, but something about the atmosphere in that place has stuck with me. Was this the place where Jesus "became sin for us" (2 Corinthians 5:21) prior to the crucifixion? Again, I do not know for sure. However, I do know that Jesus' experience in this garden has left a powerful impression on the spiritual realm—so much so that it bleeds over into the physical realm. This could be a cultivated atmosphere as well, but it seems far more focused on an event in the past than on worship and praise creating this sort of spiritual environment in the present.

Thin places can also be the result of *spiritual monuments to breakthrough* that has taken place in the past. For example, while I was attending Bethel School of Supernatural Ministry, I always saw an angel visit a certain spot in the building where the first-year school was being held. No matter what, I would see that angel at least two or three times each week. I didn't pay much attention to it, save for the fact that it seemed strange that this particular angel was always visiting the same spot. Toward the end of the year, a friend from the school asked if I ever saw an angel in that spot. He told me how he had been praying and "dreaming with God"—literally asking God to invade and sanctify his imagination as a way to hone his ability to hear, and in doing so he had "imagined" an angel in that spot. When he described what the angel looked like, I quickly realized it was identical to the angel I had been seeing!

This was enough to get me on the same page as the Holy Spirit. I asked Him what was taking place, and was pretty shocked with what I sensed Him say. He told me that someone had experienced a great breakthrough in that exact spot and the angel was visiting a spiritual monument to that breakthrough.

Somehow, this made sense. In the Old Testament, it was common to place several stones in a pile as a monument so others would remember the spiritual breakthrough that had taken place in that location. These monuments of stone were set to commemorate the occasion and show future generations what God had done. Interestingly enough, the first example of this is also found in Genesis 28, and there are many further examples throughout Scripture.

If this happened so often in the physical realm, why would the spiritual realm be any different? Do we believe that heaven really celebrates our victories? If they are celebrated, it is safe to conclude they are commemorated, especially since we see this pattern so interwoven through Scripture.

I believe that great breakthroughs can create places of increased angelic activity, regardless of whether the breakthrough is personal (Genesis 28) or corporate (Joshua 4:8).

Regardless of how a thin place is created, seers will gravitate toward them. Something about the increased spiritual activity of a cultivated atmosphere, activated atmosphere, or spiritual monument draws seers and mystics like a moth to flame. Whether these places make for easier "flow" in the anointing, or thin places simply feel more like "home" for the seer, the draw is undeniable.

I have also noticed that angelic activity has a pull toward anyone that is hungry for the supernatural. The cause of this activity doesn't matter as much as the fact that it is taking place. Those who are hungry for the supernatural things of God will almost always find themselves in one of these types of environments.

It stands to reason that if angelic activity can be drawn to a certain place for all of the reasons we have discussed, the enemy could have the same sort of pull to a particular place. I don't want to shine a spotlight on the enemy or the kingdom of darkness. Demons love attention and I don't plan to give them any. However, it is important to touch on this topic from a strategic standpoint.

A thin place can also be a place of cultivated spiritual darkness. Imagine the effect repeated actions and words can have on an area and its spiritual atmosphere. If we truly believe our words have power, what does it do when we curse a place repeatedly? My hometown was known for years in local Christian circles as a "spiritual dry spot" and a place where "there was a dark cloud." The people of God were actually reinforcing the work of the enemy with their words! I believe that every locally famous "haunted house," along with red light districts, sites of pagan worship, and even some bars (not all, but definitely some) can be thin places in their own right, just not in the sense that God intended.

The devil is a liar and a counterfeiter. Anything that God does, he will attempt to twist and use to hurt people. This means there are places where darkness manifests more readily. Feelers instantly know when they're in these sort of places; they just tend to "make the hair on the back of your neck stand up." Even non-feelers can sense these places. Ever wonder why closets can sometimes be creepy places? It's because of cultivated darkness.

A good example of this sort of place is the old barn that stood on my wife's former homestead. There is something about that barn that makes my skin crawl. It isn't just me; Cally always had a seemingly irrational fear of the old barn. From the time she was young into her adult years, she has always thought of the barn as holding a frightening presence. There are several supernatural experiences tied to this place. While neither of us have ever figured out the specifics of these experiences, I have a prophetic inkling that they had something to do with pagan rituals. Either way, releasing God's presence in a place like this can make a powerful impact. After we did this, the old barn—now torn down due to disrepair—had a much lighter spiritual atmosphere in which angelic activity was a regular occurrence and the spirit of fear was no longer present.

When we encounter places of demonic activity, there is no reason to fear, for greater is He that is in us than the spirit of this world (see 1 John 4:4). These places are simply ground to reclaim for God's Kingdom.

Remember, the Kingdom of Light naturally pushes back darkness. It may seem that the darkness is winning at times, but the mandate of every Christian is to reclaim this ground. In a very real sense we are called to create thin places where heaven can manifest, especially in places where darkness has a hold. Taking back enemy territory and creating areas of angelic activity is the ultimate victory and a central theme of Scripture! We are not only liberating the land and people from captivity; we are bringing heaven to earth.

John 5 tells a tale revolving around another thin place, that being the Pool of Bethesda. I have visited this site in Jerusalem and can confirm it is definitely a thin place. The presence of God is incredibly thick there (no doubt because of what Jesus did!), to the point that our group went to great effort to lower a few articles of jewelry into the water that remained beneath the excavation site!

The people of that day believed angelic/supernatural activity in that place was tied to healing. In the story, people with all manner of illness and disease were waiting near the water, because whenever the water was stirred they believed an angel was actually present at that moment to bring about healing. For some reason, only the first person to get into the water ever got healed, so there was something of a mad dash to get into the water and receive from heaven.

I have often wondered how they found out about this place. What did the first miracle that took place there look like? Did a crippled person fall in, just as the angel was stirring the pool? Was it merely a bit of pagan folklore that brought the people hope? Either way, the place offered hope of a chance for people to glimpse a heavenly reality. Jesus healed a man who was waiting to encounter heaven. He showed Himself superior to any atmosphere, angelic activity, pagan tradition, or thin place. When in doubt, remember that Jesus supersedes anything in the atmosphere. You are an encounter waiting to happen, no matter the setting.

When the Roman army would conquer a new territory, they would send an apostle (that's right, *apostle* is a term we have borrowed for the New Testament) to ensure that this new territory would become truly "Roman." Their goal was to impose the culture of Rome over the existing culture in the territory in order to create some sort of cohesion between the widespread segments of their sprawling empire. It was not enough for the flag of Rome to fly over a city; the city must become truly Roman at its core, to the point that the people in it began to self-identify as Roman citizens.

When we claim ground from the enemy, the same thing takes place in the spiritual realm. The atmosphere begins to shift as the kingdom of darkness vanishes and the Kingdom of Light begins to break in. We don't just occupy enemy territory; we change it to Kingdom territory where the reality of the Kingdom supersedes the former reality.

CULTIVATING THE GIFT

If you are one of the many who are hungry for more of the supernatural things of God, good! This hunger is one of driving forces that allows people to step into new experiences and new gifts of the Spirit. Seeing the gifts operate in the lives of others should create a stirring inside of you. Perhaps you see someone give an astonishingly accurate prophetic word and think to yourself, "I wish I could do that!" The good news is, you can!

1 Corinthians 12:31 says to "earnestly desire the greater gifts." The Greek word that we translate as *earnestly desire* (*zeloo*) is translated as *covet, zealously affect,* and *envy* in other New Testament verses. There is a godly jealousy that drives believers to step into spiritual gifts!

What does godly jealously look like? It's the opposite of a poverty mindset. Growing up there was probably one kid, maybe more, in your school that just seemed to get whatever they wanted. Around Christmas time you just knew they were going to be rocking whatever the "it" toy was for that season. Their parents had good jobs, or were willing to go into debt a few times a year to give good gifts.

This is you! God is a good Father who has already paid for every gift. How you reacted to the scenario above reveals your view of God and your view of yourself. If you had a negative reaction, you might want to ask God if a poverty mindset has any hold on you. If this is the case, it doesn't mean there is something wrong with you, just that your life experiences have taught you to think this way. However, this is a mindset that God desires to correct so you may see the world through His eyes.

A poverty mindset says if one person has a gift, one less gift is available for you. A Kingdom mindset says one person stepping into a gift opens the door for others to walk through to the same gift. The seers around us have walked through the door, not because they are special or super spiritual, but because they are forerunners who are clearing paths for others to follow.

We live in a culture where people are more willing to travel for impartation and to sit under anointed teachers than ever before. Sometimes, just being around people who walk in faith and blessing can be enough for that to rub off. If you desire the seer anointing, start running with seers! This is such an overlooked potential piece of the puzzle. When Saul came into the presence of the prophets, He prophesied (1 Samuel 19:24). Simply being in the presence of seers can be the push that is needed to open our eyes to the spiritual realm. Identify the seers in your sphere and seek out opportunities to spend time with them. Hear their stories. Minister alongside them. The breakthrough will come. I've seen it happen in my own life.

Do not miss an opportunity for impartation. If there are seers in your sphere, ask them to lay hands on you and pray that your eyes would be opened! Seers, don't be stingy about praying for release of the impartation of your gifts! Any time you can usher someone into the supernatural is a beautiful gift from God.

I was once on a retreat in Chico, California and ended up rooming with a couple of guys who became true friends. The first night, I looked at one of them and said something to the effect of, "I release dreams for you, in Jesus' name." He awoke in the middle of the night to God's presence, praising God with his hands raised. I would later find out that this was the first time he had encountered God to this degree.

If you're a seer, don't hesitate to receive further impartation from others who walk in the gift! Prayer is either going to unlock a gift or bring an increase to the measure of faith that drives the power of the anointing that you function under. The first time I had someone pray over me and declare that, "God was going to open my eyes to the spiritual realm"; I totally rejected the prophetic word and shrugged it off. What a mistake. I wish I had received this word as God increasing my gift, rather than thinking to myself, "I already have that." Pride will keep you from growing in what God has put inside of you. It was not long before I shifted my mindset. When someone would pray a similar prayer over me, I would quietly tell God, "I receive this increase. Allow me to see more." This never failed to bring some measure of breakthrough.

To be able to receive from young people, fresh seers, and those who you wouldn't expect to have anything to offer you requires a humility that destroys any traces of pride that may linger in the shadows of your life. A community of seers who can learn from one another and receive from one another is a ridiculous factor for multiplication! Alone you may see a certain level of breakthrough, but together you can and will change the world.

This has been said before, but I'll say it again here—don't despise beginning with using your spiritual eyes or open-eyed imagination.

This is part of the path of stepping into the seer anointing for many people. If you tend toward visual processing don't hesitate to rely on that aspect of your gift. Whether it's a closed vision, open vision, immersive vision, or spiritual sight, share what you see as long as it can be done in a way that is encouraging and edifying. This stretching of the gift will allow you to step into new territories. Think of it like lifting weights. No one can walk up to a rack of weights and throw around 250 pounds on their first outing, though I've met a few people who look as though they could. It takes years of dedication to step up to the weight that some professional lifters move with relative ease. Start small, take risks, and thank God for what you do see.

Thankfulness is a key to increase in any spiritual gift. The seer anointing is no different. In fact, it may be the number one most effective tactic to growing and cultivating the gift. I honestly believe that most people have the seeds of the seer anointing within them. Think about it, nearly everyone has seen something move in the corner of their vision, seen something in the mirror that wasn't there, or seen a shape move in the darkness at one time or another. Those who shrug it off because of fear or unbelief miss the opportunity to step further into the supernatural. When these little things happen, honor them and thank God. Share the experience with someone in your sphere. Get some encouragement to keep pressing onward. In the beginning, you'll see something from the corner of your eye, but be unable to see it when you're looking at it straight on. Through the process, you'll begin to see clearly from all angles. Just be thankful for anything you do see, as this is the first step to being trusted with more. Every increase and every experience is cause for celebration, which trains you to be a good steward of the gifts you have been given.

This is going to sound like a no-brainer, but you'd be surprised how many people miss this simple path: ask God to open your eyes. I have talked to countless people who express a desire to step into the seer anointing, but when asked if they have prayed for the gift they respond with a look of bewilderment. There is nothing wrong with asking God to open your eyes!

Being born with a gift grants authority, but hunger draws the anointing. We need a generation of people who walk in this dynamic combination. Authority and anointing are both powerful, but when a person has honed the craft of their gift (authority) and purposefully kept the fire of hunger for increase burning (anointing) they will not only walk in a greater measure of their gift, they will step into a realm of impartation that is critical to the equipping of the saints. To put it bluntly, our generation must be capable in *gifting* and powerful in *experience* if we are to see global transformation go from the seed of a dream to the over-abundant fruit of reality.

Physical health *really* needs to be addressed while talking about cultivating the seer anointing, or any spiritual gift for that matter. In the West, we have an understanding of ourselves that is lacking when compared with the traditional Hebraic understanding. I'm sure you have heard the breakdown that you *are* a soul and you *have* a body and a spirit. Our Messianic brothers and sisters are far more likely to believe that you *are* a triune being—body, soul, and spirit making up the fullness of your being. I've even heard the Star of David explained as two triangles, one facing up and one facing down. Father, Son, and Spirit facing the earth and body, soul, and spirit facing heaven. God and man—two triune beings in relationship. If we take an Eastern view of our being, which we should, seeing as we are part of an Eastern religion called Christianity, then our bodies begin to matter more and become something more than just "flesh" that needs to be put in line.

Part of my journey has been overcoming spiritual and emotional trials that led to my misusing and mistreating my body. At one point, I weighed 340 pounds and would lose my breath just by walking up a flight of stairs. Between the birth of my daughter and receiving a massive revelation of my own value and worth, I began a journey of bettering my health and losing the weight. As I write this paragraph, I have lost more than 100 pounds and am on track to lose more!

Aside from being able to fit into my old clothes and being able to keep up with my toddler, there have been a few strange fringe benefits to my weight loss. The spiritual gifts I walk in have begun to function better as my physical body comes into alignment with its original design. I know this sounds crazy, but I have more dreams, see more visions, see in the Spirit more easily, you name it. It's all functioning with more regularity and clarity since I have begun taking better care of myself, and I imagine this will only increase as my health continues to improve!

There is an undeniable link between the health of the body and the health of the mind and spirit. If we are truly triune beings, which I believe we are, damage or neglect to one part of us can limit how the other parts function. Every mentally ill person I've known has had issues with caring for themselves (body) and having a healthy relationship with God (spirit). Every person I've known who harbors anger toward God has had issues with physical illness (body) and difficulty in looking at the profound philosophical and theological reasoning for His existence and nature (mind). Now, I know there are handicaps that make it difficult for people to bring their bodies into better physical condition, but those are extreme cases that I am not lumping into the norm. As a general rule, doing what you are able to do physically (whether that's Crossfit training or lifting a couple of soup cans and walking around the house a few times a day) to better your health will have a positive effect on your ability to hear God's voice and tap into the gifts.

If you are already a seer, it is my greatest desire that you will be intentional to help others step into the gift. Elitism has no place in the Kingdom, and if you're looking at the prospect of an increase in the number of seers with any sense of fear or dread, you have probably allowed your gift to be a much larger part of your identity than is healthy. Seeing into the Spirit is a part of who you are, but it is not the sum total of who you are! Seers have a responsibility to cultivate and reproduce their gifts in the lives of others, in effect multiplying what they have been given freely.

I stumbled across a pretty amazing piece of wisdom while having a conversation with an old friend named Tobias. He was talking about leading an evangelism group at his church when the following words just "fell" out of my mouth: *Pour into the hungry ones, invite the interested ones along, engage the apathetic, and ignore the hostile.* Since then, this has become my personal life strategy!

The hungry ones need someone to pour into them. They desire "more," and you have likely experienced just what they are after. Who better to guide them into the fullness of the Spirit?! Regular encouragement goes a lot farther than you might think. Even to refocus the hungry one back to the Kingdom and their goals can be enough to bring about breakthrough. Ask what they're seeing, tell them what you're seeing. It will increase their hunger for the supernatural and bring about growth.

If someone is merely "interested," pouring into them might be a bit overwhelming. Inviting them into the experience of a group of seers and hungry people can be just enough for the enthusiasm of others rub off on them. Hearing the stories of seers and seeing the breakthrough as people step into the gift is electrifying and exciting. People who are interested but unsure won't stay in that place long. The draw of seeing what God is doing is magnetic.

Engaging the apathetic is not a call to debate the value or even existence of the seer anointing. You cannot debate a person into changing their mind on the supernatural. Even if you could, a person who is talked into something can probably be talked out of it. You will likely meet a fellow brother or sister at some point who does not believe the gifts of the Spirit are alive and active today. Engage them with the heart of the Father. Tell them of the gifts or callings you see on their lives. Engage in prophetic ministry while they are in the room. Show them the fruit and impact that a word from God can have on the individual and on the church. Sometimes, these folks will come around. Other times, they won't. Remember, some of the folks who have arrived at this place have seen or been the victim of others abusing the gifts of the Spirit for their own personal gain or to "put on a show." In these instances, it is particularly important to show them where the things you walk in are found in Scripture and the fruit that these gifts bring. It's hard to argue with good fruit and changed lives! Above all else, protect relational connection—even if that means you have to agree to disagree. It is sad to see fellowship broken over spiritual gifts when both parties share a deep love for Jesus. The Body cannot survive if it is cut apart. Avoid the temptation toward elitism if someone rejects the gifts you walk in and focus on maintaining the relationship.

If someone is hostile toward the supernatural and the seer anointing, forget about them. I don't mean refuse to pray for them or to leave them out of what God is doing. What I mean is don't make it your focus to win them over or convert them to your way of thinking. At that point, you are playing junior Holy Spirit, and it's His job to deal with these sorts of things, not ours. He is good at His job and knows what He is doing. Pray for the skeptics, that God would invite them into the gift and into the supernatural realm. These people can sometimes be the most powerful allies once they come around (like modern-day Paul's). It can take years, but they will be the most zealous seekers of the supernatural once they catch the fire. In the meantime, let the Holy Spirit do His work and don't try to argue with those who are hostile.

It is paramount for us to remember that love is the canvas that our faith is painted upon. This is true for pastoral gifts, healing, miracles, and the seer anointing. You name it, without love it ceases to be of any real value. The seer without love is without a power source. It's like the batteries have been taken out. There is still something of substance, but it just doesn't function like it was intended. Without love, the seer anointing is mere "spiritual surveillance." You can gather all of the information in the world, but it can easily end up as evidence for accusation rather than intelligence for Kingdom victory when love falls off the radar.

MAKING A CHURCH SEER-FRIENDLY

One of the most profound experiences I've ever had was at a worship service that took place during a disaster relief training. Jay Baylor was there teaching prophecy, healing, and deliverance (yeah, it was a wild training!). He took the mic during the service and did something that would forever change my life. Jay said, "To any seers in this room, on behalf of the Church. I'm sorry. We haven't valued your gift and we haven't made room for you, and I'm sorry." I was in the back of the room, weeping as healing bathed my spirit. A pastor had the courage to address and own a grievance committed by the Church at large. The time that followed was incredible. The handful of seers that were in the training were asked to come forward and describe what they were seeing right at that moment. I got to see my brothers and sisters call out the gold in people as they were honored and exhorted to function in their gift. Many were set free that day.

Making an environment seer-friendly is a bit more complicated than one might like to believe. Accepting the seer anointing corporately seems to draw a line in the sand, even more so than teaching on miracles, signs, and wonders. Once you cross that line there is no going back, but it's so worth the risk! I don't believe it is necessary for every church to apologize for missing the chance to disciple and make room for the seers among them. I think Jay was led by God to do what he did so I (among others) could receive some long overdue healing. God saw that I had been suppressing a big part of who I was when I ministered, and I think He finally decided enough was enough.

In a church setting, a good start for incorporating the seer anointing in a worship service is by using the pulpit. Fellow pastors, if you want seers to be at home in your church, start including this anointing when you speak on spiritual gifts. The list of spiritual gifts in the New Testament is in no way exhaustive. If it were, there would be more gifts available under the Old Covenant than the New Covenant! That is hard to believe.

If common language begins to include the seer anointing, it will be easier to integrate this gift into worship services, ministry times, and the community at large. One caveat I'd like to include is this: If you're *not* a seer, please be careful when preaching about the seer anointing. Most of the seers around you have possessed this gift from birth. Though it is not the sum total of their identity, it cannot help but be a part of who they are. It would be something like a male minister preaching a message about what it's like to be a woman. He can research all he wants, but he can never truly know her experience. Teaching the biblical foundations is awesome, but unless the Holy Spirit is really stirring you to dive deeper, stop there. God will bring a seer into your midst that can teach what the congregation needs to hear. Better yet, bring in a trusted prophetic teacher to instruct, model, and activate the seer anointing in your congregation.

Finally, honor the gift and make room for it to function. If you are in an atmosphere where prophetic people can share words during worship, make sure that seers are included. Two different gifted people may receive similar revelations, but the seer sharing a vision or experience will impact a different segment than those impacted by the prophetic word going forth. This way, the revelation is being communicated to maximum effect.

Include seers in prophetic teams, intercession teams, and please, please, have your seers in deliverance ministry if it's their call (it usually is to some degree). The most valuable asset in warfare is intelligence. Seers bring this to the table.

Another caveat needs to be addressed. Many seers begin experiencing demonic attacks at a young age. Some will start to associate deliverance/warfare ministry with their identity. (This is even more prevalent in settings where the seer anointing isn't given free expression.) Being in the battle 24/7 is exhausting but allowing the battle to become your identity is the real killer. Make sure the seers around you know you see them as more than their gifting.

To the seers: know that God has given you an amazing gift, but you are a son or daughter first and foremost. That is your identity. Being a seer is simply another tool on your belt. No matter how strong the gift, how anointed the call, how favored the office, you cannot become a hammer any more than you can become the gift. I promise, as you place your identity in your sonship your gifts will flourish. They will flow out of who you are, not define who you are.

Making room for seers is not an overnight shift. It requires time, strategy, and risk. The endgame is beautiful because it looks like another part of the Body is reattached. When the full Body of Christ is expressed, we see more of who Jesus is manifest among us. The world is dying for an encounter with the living God, and the seers have insight into the supernatural realm that we must not discount or overemphasize. Experience has been downplayed for so long. It is time that we allow the experiential component back into the Church.

CHAPTER 4

————

MY LITTLE SEER

long imagined what it would have been like to grow up trained and equipped in the gift I didn't fully understand. To be a seer from birth who was honored early and allowed to grow and experiment alongside others who understood.

I never dreamed I'd get to see this play out within my lifetime. Times are changing and the Church is starting to embrace the prophetic and spiritual realms in ways that give me great hope.

My daughter, Serenity, is an absolute wonder. She's also been a case study of the theory that spiritual gifts and anointings flow down through generational lines. "Ren" is bright eyed, inquisitive, and beautiful. She's also a full-blown seer. I noticed her, at a very early age, reacting to stimulus in the spiritual environment, but I assumed that meant she was a feeler like her mother. It wasn't until I woke her up from a nap one fateful afternoon that I learned the truth. As I lay next to her, she pointed out the doorway into the room we affectionately called the "second bedroom" though it was more of a storage space.

She could have been pointing at anything, but I was seeing an angel in the room at the exact moment she pointed. I watched this familiar angel slowly leave the room. To my astonishment, my daughter removed the pacifier from her mouth, waved to the angel, and said "bye-bye" rather loudly! That was only the beginning.

I began occasionally asking Ren what she saw in a room, only after I'd taken some time to note where spiritual activity was happening. Without fail, with a near 100% accuracy rate, she has told me that she's seeing angels in the same places as I. This came without coaching; I simply ask her if she sees anything in the room.

Ren, like all young seers, also sees the occasional demon. Once when we were living in California, I was putting her down for the night when she suddenly became unusually active. She was actually pushing herself up on the bed in terror. I asked her what was going on, and she pointed to the corner and said, "Scary guy, daddy!" There in the corner, stood a demon.

My initial reaction was to go after that spirit. It was something of a symbol of the pain that I'd experienced as a young seer without any guidance. Then it hit me. I could train Ren up instead of taking out my frustration. That was the way to win. I asked her, "Honey, do you remember who Jesus is? His name is above every other name. So, if you see a scary guy, just tell them to go away in Jesus' name. Then they have to leave." She looked long at me, then turned to the demon and said, "In Jesus' name, go away, scary guy!" It left, and the atmosphere in the room was instantly peaceful. Moreover, Ren rolled over and was fast asleep within minutes. It wasn't just her victory that day, it was mine. The cycle of training her in her gift had increased even more, and I'm excited to see what we can do with a generation of seers who grow up embracing their gift rather than running from it or trying to hide it.

I've talked with a few individuals who are not seers but their children are. It's amazing to see the way these parents are learning to embrace the gift in their children rather than pushing it under the rug and pretending that it isn't happening. I spoke with a mother and daughter in a local Methodist church a few years ago. The little girl was, at the time, somewhere between the ages of four and six and she was telling her mother all about how she was seeing angels and having conversations with Jesus. To my surprise, her mother was not just supportive, she genuinely thought the gift her little girl carried was amazing! This generation, more than any other, will witness the seers coming out of the shadows and into their place as a necessary part of the Body of Christ.

RAISING A SEER

It is more common than you might imagine for a seer to have parents who do not walk in the gift, and there are practical ways to steward the gifts that God has given to your children. The most basic strategy is to talk to your children about what they are seeing, and do so without any shame or disbelief. A parent has an incredible level of influence over their child's spiritual development. I know my mother didn't understand what I was walking in, but she never made me feel ashamed of the things I shared. Had she, I may have just turned my back on what I was seeing. Had my parents known that the seer anointing existed, I could have been spared a great deal of difficulty. When I met my wife, I began sharing the things I was experiencing openly for the first time. Talking about these experiences is so important. Ask your child to describe in detail what they are seeing. Help them to dig deeper. Ask about why they are seeing it. Help them to discern the greater purpose of the gift.

A parent can also help their child take risks. This doesn't mean that daddy forces their little seer into the limelight to share their visions. It does mean that parents can lovingly create an environment where it is safe for their children to share the things they are seeing. Whether this means passing notes with the pastor or delivering a personal word to a man or woman who has been highlighted, the seer anointing can be cultivated at a far younger age than we realize. What harm would it do to ask a child if they want to bless anyone after a church service? What person would refuse prayer from a child?! I've seen children serve very effectively on evangelism teams, as they are fearless and hear God better than most would think!

We have given our daughter the opportunity to join in with us when we pray for the sick and prophesy over people. On one occasion, our family was visiting with a neighbor and friend before we left California to return to Wisconsin. We prayed over our friend before leaving, and my wife was struck with the idea to ask Serenity if she saw anything. Ren paused for just a second, and said "butterflies" with a knowing nod toward the woman. Our friend stared at us in a state of awe, and then told us that butterflies had been a picture for her of the transformation that was currently taking place in her life. Ren hit a home run, simply because her mother gave her the opportunity instead of having a "children should be seen and not heard" mindset.

I've heard accounts of native tribes that required children to sit on the council. As the story goes, the elders were aware that a child will approach a situation with different eyes and this can be the edge that helps to find a solution. Does the Church do this, or are our children seen but not heard? Their gifts go dormant if they aren't utilized. I'm not advising that we wantonly put our kids to work, but they can participate in ministry along with us! Their insight could lead to significant breakthrough.

In 2 Chronicles 34 and 2 Kings 21, we read the story of Josiah becoming King at eight years of age. King at eight! I believe one of the reasons his reign was so successful was because he came into responsibility so early. He still had to be mentored and molded into the position, but in all reality the weight of the crown strengthened him rather than crushing him. Our kids are born carrying more authority than the devil will ever have. The sooner we encourage them to walk in it, the better. Insulating our children from the reality of the Kingdom isn't doing them any favors. In fact, it's stifling their ability to learn to flow with the Holy Spirit. Should a child lead a congregation? Probably not. Should they have a voice? There is no other choice that looks like honor. We are not honoring the next generation unless we allow them to participate. In a culture that removes responsibility from children and gives out free participation prizes, a Church culture that hands children responsibility is a true light in the darkness.

Children hear the Gospel in all of its glory and they have no reason to doubt its efficacy. Their faith is naturally childlike! They need to be trained to doubt, not the other way around. Controlling them isn't the answer, and neither is curbing their enthusiasm. We can and should raise up a generation that isn't surprised when a person is supernaturally touched by God. In fact, we can raise up a generation that is genuinely surprised when their risk doesn't lead to an invasion of heaven. I remember the first time Ren prayed for an "owie" and it didn't get healed. She was so confused! She'd already seen several miracles by partnering with Jesus. This time, she prayed for a scrape on her leg and it didn't disappear. She looked at me with an incredible degree of confusion. What was going on? Why wasn't the owie gone? She touched mystery that day without losing her faith. She bore the crown without being crushed by it.

I had a vision in February of 2015 that I will never forget. I was standing in the back of a room full of worshippers. It looked like a standard worship service, but everyone in attendance was a child. I remember worshipping for a short time, then asking God, "Why children? What are you trying to tell me?" At that moment, every child in the room turned toward me and I got my answer. Their eyes were glowing with the most radiant, pure, white light. The Holy Spirit then spoke to me: "I am raising up a generation of seers, and they need to be trained and equipped to push back the darkness." This moment was a profound marking for me, and probably a motivation for the writing this book. These little seers are already walking among us, and we have the duty, the honor, and the responsibility to raise them up to their destiny.

THE CALL TO SPIRITUAL WARFARE

The seer will probably have some sort of call to spiritual warfare on their life. This is where it seems like the enemy overplays his hand. For starters, "warfare" is probably a bad term to describe what we do as believers. Our foe has been defeated, once and for all, two thousand years ago, beginning with the cross and continuing until "every enemy is made His footstool" (Hebrews 10:13). The term "warfare" conveys a struggle, when the reality should look more like stepping over a conquered enemy. If a seer has seen spiritual attack as a child, there is a good chance that they'll be unwilling to stand idly by when attack is levied against those around them later in life. This is a good thing. Advancing the Kingdom doesn't just look like deliverance and clearing out territorial spirits. Remember that worship and intercession are valuable weapons against the enemy. Some of my most memorable moments of intercession were gathering with other seers and praying strategically based on visions, cues, and spiritual sight. There's something amazing about watching the gifts of prophecy begin to amplify as visions and angelic activity lead to focused prayers that cut to the heart of a stronghold or even a regional principality.

There is a layer of covert warfare that I wish every seer would take to heart. I was once in a church service where the lid felt like it was about to blow off of the place. The energy and expectancy in the meeting was growing rapidly. Either God was about to move, or we were about to be disappointed. At least that's what it felt like. When the pastor took the stage to preach something was wrong. It was like the fire in the room began to sputter. At that moment, I saw a demon prowling across the stage, looking like a big cat hunting its prey. As it got closer to the pastor, his message became disjointed. It was almost like this confusing spirit was affecting his mind just by moving into closer and closer proximity. I had the thought to stand up and shout at the demon. (Don't do this unless God is clearly calling you! Disturbance and distraction are rarely the plans of the Kingdom.) I prayed for a second, then said under my breath, "I cancel your assignment, demon. Leave now, in Jesus name." The spirit actually made eye contact with me, then let out a low growl and sauntered away from him. It didn't get far, because an angel pounced on that spirit and dragged it from the space. The fire was instantly back in the atmosphere. Better still, the pastor paused for a second, then delved right back into the message with a new cohesion and a fresh energy. It rocked everyone in the room—including me!

The seer gets to be a silent partner with ministry and a silent guardian in the corporate setting. Being privy to the activity of the enemy is an amazing advantage. As you walk in this, you'll notice that demons will often avoid your presence just because they recognize the measure of authority you carry. As Bill Johnson says, "You spot 'em, you got 'em." This is literally true for the seer. Any time you see a demon manifest itself, you have an opportunity to cast it out. And it's easier to cast a demon out of an *atmosphere* than to cast it out of a *person* (not to say that deliverance is difficult; it's not). Think of it like finding a tick on the ground vs. finding a tick tha has already dug into your skin. One is a matter of stepping on it and continuing forward. Any time the devil is prowling around, trying to shake up the atmosphere, he should be looking over his shoulder in fear of a seer.

Spiritual warfare isn't just about shutting down the forces of darkness. It's also about adding support and strength to the forces of light. Angela West, a small group pastor at BSSM, posed a question I had never thought of after I recounted a supernatural experience I had during worship. She said, in her typical British motherly tone, "Next time it happens, ask Holy Spirit how to partner with what He's doing in the room."

I was floored. That thought had never occurred to me! But if we really are the Body of Christ, then the work of the Kingdom belongs to us. Perhaps God is using these manifestations to help guide us into His strategy for victory. For example, we use the phrase "open heaven" a lot. In a broad sense, we are all living under an open heaven—God is present and willing to work on our behalf, no matter what comes our way. But in a more focused sense, I believe that we can come into an atmosphere of the presence of Jesus that makes manifest this reality. What I usually see in those moments looks something like a night sky, filled with stars and colors, bleeding through whatever roof or sky I'm currently under. What I've noticed is when I see that particular cue, it usually means God is going to bring healing and encounter people in a personal way. However, our ability to partner with God and the forces of heaven doesn't end there. In fact, this may be the most basic piece of understanding as to how to receive and carry out commissions from a God who values interaction with us more than He does perfection in service.

Ask the Holy Spirit what obedience looks like in the moment. Partnering with heaven won't always make a ton of sense. Other times, it will be exactly what you would expect. I know I have been in settings where God called me to simply walk around and speak prophetic words over people He highlighted. I've also been in situations in which I felt God asking me to perform strange prophetic acts, like throwing stones into a pond and declaring trials, sin, and shame drowned at the bottom of the ocean like the pebbles. I've watched prophetic people march around a room before a worship night, dancing and singing and declaring the walls to fall down like Jericho. I think that Jesus just loves His time with us, and sometimes He chooses our childlike faith and obedience to bring about the riches of the Kingdom.

WATCHERS IN THE HOUSE

There is a definite training and development that goes into the use of any gift from God, but what about training the community at large to flow with the Holy Spirit? Seeing into the spiritual realm is critical for this sort of shaping and training to take place, not to mention it provides significant and instant feedback. However, this needs to be said: Not everything you see needs to be shared, nor is it relevant to share everything you see. Because the seer anointing has been so overlooked in mainstream Christianity, it is possible to swing the pendulum far to the opposite end of the spectrum, landing in an unhealthy place that looks far too much like a "seer show" every time the Body is gathered together. Walk the journey out with the Holy Spirit, and honor the environment of the room. You may feel a burning desire to share about an angel you just saw, but if the leadership of a house don't think it's time to share this corporately, it isn't time. Honor begets honor and accelerates Kingdom advancement.

More often than not the seer anointing is useful simply to chart out whether the church got it right, or missed the mark in flowing with the Holy Spirit. Think of it like the process of learning to hear the voice of God. When you get it right, you pay attention to what was going on mentally, physically, and emotionally when He spoke. That way you can know when you're hearing Him clearly in the future. Organizations with seers in their sphere have an edge in the same process. For example, my wife and I recently attended an evening worship service. During worship, I fell into a trance and saw a vision of a man kneeling in front of a large metal dam. The dam had a crack down the middle, but no water was flowing. The man, whom I only saw from the back, reached up and pulled the two pieces apart with his bare hands. Suddenly, water started to flow! When I opened my eyes, I could still see the river flowing through the sanctuary. It came from the stage and turned off to my right before heading right down the center of the room.

Moments later, one of the leaders came to the stage and spoke out a word of knowledge, calling a few women forward for ministry. They walked straight to the spot where the water was pouring out. As if this wasn't confirmation enough, the pastor called Cally forward to minister to one of the ladies along with his wife and they walked right to the spot where the river took a bend. It wasn't until a week later that I recounted the experience to anyone. I had no inclination to share what I saw, nor did it seem that the Holy Spirit was leading me to do so. What I saw was just a confirmation that those leading the service had partnered with what God was doing.

What would it look like if every ministry had a handful of seers who they could simply check in with either during or after something outside of the ordinary happened in the church? Seers can change the tide of a floundering service into a powerful experience of heaven simply by using their gift to sort out what is happening in the spiritual realm and partnering with God to see what He desires to do. They can also recap the spiritual events of a ministry time so that the leaders can hone their own ability to follow the Spirit in corporate settings.

Seers get to watch a real-time highlight reel of what is taking place in the spiritual realm! Sports teams pour over the video of their past games to see potential missteps, triumphs, and new strategies based on how their team and the opposition squared off. If a seer has a good memory (or does what I have done and begin carrying around a notebook and pen), this sort of thing can occur after any service, outreach, or ministry event. Look at what happened in the spiritual realm before and after events in the physical realm. This can lead to new strategies and shifts the focus toward what God is doing rather than what man can do.

Certain passages in Isaiah and Ezekiel have created an unhealthy "watchmen" identity and mentality in some believers. (See Isaiah 21 and Ezekiel 33.) These passages have been interpreted by some to mean prophetic people should constantly be on the lookout for something bad to happen, almost as though it is their responsibility to sound the alarm. Almost any Old Testament passage can bring confusion if it is not tempered with the revelation of who God is that the New Testament brings.

In the ancient world, watchmen were vital to the function of a city. They would take their place on the tower and watch for enemy threats, thieves, and even animals that would damage the valuable crops growing outside the walls. The watchmen is a beautiful picture of the Old Testament prophet. The only trouble is this: it is impossible to get New Covenant results from an Old Covenant reality.

The New Testament paints a very different picture of a "watcher" in Luke 15:11-32. The parable of the Prodigal Son points to the fact that the Father saw His son a long way off and ran to restore him. He was watching for His son. To be a watchman on the wall in the New Covenant means we are watching for the returning prodigals that we might partner with God for their restoration. This doesn't mean we don't assess threats in the spiritual realm, but it does highlight the importance of separating those threats from *people*. Maybe your declaration and prayer was the key that drew the prodigal back from the pig pen, but your readiness to encourage and love them will be the true beginning of restoration.

INTERACTING WITH
THE SPIRITUAL REALM

The spiritual realm is the superior realm in our existence. What happens *here* is a reflection of what is going on *there*, not vice-versa. We are to make an impact on the spiritual realm. If that weren't the case, then deliverance wouldn't be possible. Blessing wouldn't be possible. None of these things could be a reality. Interaction with the spiritual realm isn't just a *possibility*, it is our *mandate*. This should create a hunger for more supernatural experiences, and for an even greater revelatory awareness.

Hebrews 1:14 is an intriguing verse when it comes to our relationship with angels. Understanding this passage changed the way that I approached ministry, the spiritual realm, and the advancement of the Kingdom. "Are they (*angels*) not all ministering spirits, sent out to render service for the sake of those who will inherit salvation?"(Hebrews 1:14, emphasis added). This certainly seems to point toward a relationship with angels that goes far beyond what we've been taught. It's a bit like missing a piece of our spiritual inheritance. Now to be fair, it wasn't like this verse inspired a new season of interaction with the spiritual realm. It sort of made my encounters with angels "legal."

I had always seen angels, but I went through a season where there seemed to be more angels spending time around us than usual, and these angels just seemed to be standing around. They weren't keeping watch. They weren't carrying out assignments. They just seemed to be waiting for something. It went on like this for weeks. It was comforting knowing that they were there, but something about it was still strange and tense. We sometimes overlook the obvious in these sorts of seasons. I was no different, as in it took way longer than it should have for me to ask the Holy Spirit what was going on!

The response was shocking. I heard God say, "They're waiting for orders." This didn't seem to make sense. As I was trying to process through it, I heard Him say it again. I don't know if it's like this for everyone, but I get frustrated sometimes when I'm searching something out. I think God likes it, maybe the same way that I find my wife adorable when she gets irritated with my occasionally erratic behavior. Maybe He's teaching me something through it! I said something along the lines of, "Then give them something to do."

The reply came as clear as any word I've ever heard. "You do it." I was absolutely floored. The King of the Universe had just told me to interact with the angelic in a way that I'd never dreamed possible. This assignment came with what I can only describe as fear and trembling.

So, I started trying it out. I didn't want to be presumptuous with requests like finding my television remote. I started with things like preparing the hearts of people at our ministry, or drawing provision. The angels who I asked to draw provision disappeared. I didn't see them again until the next day. As I was walking into our church, I saw those same angels coming and going, and a pile of what I can only describe as treasure building at the door of the building. Nobody ever wrote a massive check to our ministry, at least not at the time of this writing, but it wasn't too long before our family was offered a year in Redding to attend BSSM at no cost to us. The provision that those angels brought ushered in the most radical breakthrough experience of my life.

Interacting with the spiritual realm also effects how we do warfare and deliverance. It would make sense that having extra intel and being able to effectively communicate with the angelic would grant some advantage. I remember doing deliverance ministry once and being at the absolute end of my rope. I'd done nearly everything I knew to do. If deliverance starts to move past a certain point in time and energy, I'd rather not keep fighting. When it comes to deliverance sessions that last three to four hours, I'd rather take a break and regroup than keep on pressing. This wasn't getting us anywhere, and it was taking longer than I wanted. It was then that I noticed angels standing on my right and my left. I looked at them, then asked, "Got any ideas?" I watched, in shock, as the angels grabbed the demon and dragged it off of the person. I would think I was imagining it but the person stopped manifesting instantly. Since then, I've seen this happen repeatedly. Angels are built for warfare and we get to work with them to take back territory from the kingdom of darkness.

I used to describe angels as the "tank" of the heavenly army, but that's not quite accurate. They're probably something closer to attack helicopters. When it comes to warfare in the physical realm, one of the most devastating things that troops on the ground can do is call in air support. The tide of a battle can be turned with the arrival of just one plane or helicopter! The same is true in spiritual warfare. If we call in just one angel a radical shift can occur, let alone calling in the hundreds and thousands that are available to us as sons and daughters of God.

I know that this is a strange topic, but I don't think that this sort of thing was lost on the early Church, as angels are a constant feature of the book of Acts.

Acts chapter twelve is one such piece of scripture. Peter is arrested and imprisoned. This is during a season of intense persecution in which Herod is mistreating the Church to please the religious "old guard." It's apparent that Herod is going to make a spectacle of Peter, and presumably have him put to death.

In the night, Peter is sleeping between two soldiers and bound with two chains. Suddenly, things get wild. "And behold, an angel of the Lord suddenly appeared and a light shone in the cell; and he struck Peter's side and woke him up, saying, 'Get up quickly.' And his chains fell off his hands" (v. 7).

The angel touches Peter to wake him, then leads him out of the prison in a manner that feels like a supernatural action film. But it gets even more amazing! In verses 12-17, Peter goes to the house of Mary, the mother of John-Mark, and knocks on the door. Rhoda, the servant girl, runs and tells the people that are gathered to pray that Peter has arrived. They were probably praying for his release! They argue that he isn't there, but their argument is wildly telling. They say, "It is his angel" (v. 15) but nobody is running to see the angel! Their response is very much like a specific angel, assigned to Peter, is coming around (perhaps looking for him), and that's about as exciting as a stray cat poking through the trash bin! If an angel were manifesting itself outside of a person's home today, there'd be a line for miles to catch a glimpse. This leads me to believe that this sort of thing was commonplace for the early Church.

Since this season, angels have become a ridiculously common part of our lives. My daughter sees them constantly and sometimes says things that leave our jaws on the ground. After my aforementioned encounter on the Sea of Galilee (the one in which I spoke with my departed grandfather), an angel with dark skin and black wings started showing up in the normal group I'd see coming and going from our sphere. I told Cally about it after it seemed to linger for a few weeks. Around the same time, we started finding black feathers in the house. Cally and I never spoke of it in front of our daughter. One day, we were having supper with some old friends and Serenity had to use their bathroom. On their mirror was a sticker with angel on it. Ren looked up at it and said, "Momma, that an angel." My wife replied in the affirmative, but Ren kept going. "That not look like our angel. Our angel dirty."

"What do you mean, honey?" Cally replied. "Do you mean a color?" By this point Cally had gotten pretty good at sifting through the occasional train wreck of hurried two-year-old dialogue. It wasn't long before she had her answer.

"Our angel black," Ren replied. This absolutely floored Cally. Serenity had seen the same angel that I'd seen since my time in Israel!

Just before we left for Bethel, another strange encounter took place. My wife had just gone upstairs to put Serenity down for the evening while I was downstairs working on something or other. Less than half an hour later, I heard Cally full-on running down the stairs. I rushed into the kitchen to see what was going on. Serenity was crying and Cally had a look of terror on her face. Ren had seen something upstairs and it so unsettled her that she began to cry and scream, all the while pointing toward the closed door that led into the hallway. When Cally made up her mind to come and get me to help sort things out, she felt a presence literally chase her through the hallway and down the stairs.

Demonic manifestation was nothing new at this point, but something felt different about this incident. Either way, I went upstairs to see what had caused such a disturbance. I walked up the stairs and down the narrow hallway to our bedroom, where I sat on the bed and waited for something to happen. It wasn't long before I saw something straight out of a horror movie coming down the hallway toward me. As fear attempted to enter my heart (and I say "attempted" because it was painfully obvious that this was an external attack not born in my own spirit) the word *principality* flashed through my mind.

Ephesians 6 is the chapter I have studied the most in reference to principalities, but the title is given to both forces of light (Ephesians 3:10-11) and forces of darkness (Colossians 2:15). It seems that in both the angelic and the demonic realms, there is a sort of hierarchy of authority. I believe principalities are simply a territorial spirit that has authority over a region, and this was one such spirit. When the word flashed through my mind, it was like a special grace for the moment was released. I looked at the thing, which was now within a foot or two of my face, and chuckled aloud as it continued to move toward me. Internally, I was trying to sort out what the strategy was. Externally, this amazing grace/faith thing was terribly exciting! I was actually happy to have drawn the ire of the enemy! It was like being ready and equipped for battle in a way I have not often experienced.

It was then that it hit me. The room was full of angels. I turned my back on the principality and told the angels (there were three or four of them), "Guys, I don't have time for this today. Could you take care of it?" Like missiles, the angels shot after the thing, which fled like a rabbit with hounds on its tail. We never saw it again.

Imagine the impact on the world if a majority of the Church could catch this simple revelation that the enemy isn't just defeated, he is powerless! For too long, the people of God have allowed the devil to eat their proverbial lunch because they don't live out two simple truths:

1. You have all authority in Christ.
2. The devil has absolutely none.

CHAPTER 5

INTERACTING WITH GOD

This heading may seem a little strange. When I say "interacting with God," I don't just mean reading the Bible or praying (though our understanding of prayer is fairly narrow, and revelation on the topic could probably illuminate our experience). Encountering God is not a new topic, but the supernatural encounter of Father, Son, and Holy Spirit is something that changes the lives of individuals and drives the revival culture that we so desperately desire. God is literally infinite, but our experience tends to be finite. This is because we try and apply our limitations to God rather than expect His limitlessness to overshadow and swallow up our finite nature.

God is everywhere. This is a key tenant of our understanding of Deity. I would go so far as to say that creation exists within God. That said, God can choose to specifically manifest Himself beyond the omnipresent Presence. For example, the Father and the Holy Spirit specifically manifested in Luke 3:22, "and the Holy Spirit descended in bodily form like a dove, and a voice came out of heaven, 'You are My beloved Son, in You I am well-pleased.'" At the Transfiguration in Matthew 17, Jesus manifests His deity—fully God and fully Man, but He chose to function as a man in perfect relationship with the

Holy Spirit instead of powering on with the advantage of Deity (Philippians 2:6). In this moment, Jesus showed the disciples what His Deity looked like. It was a specific manifestation of King Jesus.

When my daughter was born the doctors recommended something I'd never heard of before: skin to skin contact. It sounded a little weird, but I wasn't going to pass up the chance to cuddle with my little girl. So, we would strip Serenity down and I would take off my shirt and lay her right on my chest. She was swallowed up in my core. This is the way that we exist in the Presence of God at every moment. A general manifestation of God in creation. However, there are also specific manifestations, which are simply interactions with God beyond the general. Serenity experienced me during skin to skin, but when I chose to hug her, kiss her, or tickle her, she had an experience of my nature that went beyond just existing in my presence.

These types of manifestations are still happening today. When God chooses to reveal Himself it is a powerful and life-changing event. There is also something to the differences in the ways God chooses to manifest. Father, Son, and Holy Spirit are one, yet they are also distinct. This means the ways we experience them are different, yet always share a common thread. This is the mystery we spend our lives trying to unravel. We are talking about encountering God! It is impossible to encounter God and remain the same. Change, healing, impartation, and all manner of glory are all released when God specifically shows up on the scene. These are some observations I have made over the years when it comes to the specific manifestations of God.

When the Father specifically manifests, it is a weighty experience of glory. (See Genesis 17:3, Numbers 14:5, Joshua 5:13-15, and even Matthew 17:6.) The accounts of people falling face down in the presence of God are numerous throughout Scripture. I believe this is, in part, because of the weightiness of who the Father is. On more than one occasion I have been in a worship setting and seen what looked like a glorious and ornate train filling the room (Isaiah 6:1). The Presence was suddenly thick (like oil) and I found myself falling on my face almost involuntarily. Many others in the room respond in the same manner when this particular manifestation occurs.

Something about the Father compels us to go prostrate. It may be that it has to do with His holiness. The Son and the Holy Spirit are all holy as well, but it does seem like it is a specific side of Deity expressed through the Father. Nowhere in the Scripture are people called to remove their sandals in the presence of Jesus or the Holy Spirit, washing the disciples' feet notwithstanding. In Exodus 3:5 and again in Joshua 5:15, the call is given to remove shoes in the presence of the Father. The phrase "holy ground" is used here, too. Something about the presence of the Father consecrates a place, a person, a region.

Encountering the Holy Spirit reveals yet another aspect of the God we serve. The best picture of the manifest presence of the Holy Spirit is found in the Acts 2 account of Pentecost. Here we see the Holy Spirit manifest as fire above the heads of those gathered. The Spirit also distributes gifts like tongues, prophecy, etc. Verse 13 holds a key to our understanding. It reads, "But others were mocking and saying, 'they are full of sweet wine.'" *Sweet wine* is probably the best description of the joy of the Spirit's presence. Many have misunderstood these verses to think that the fact that the disciples were speaking in other tongues was what led observers to surmise that they were drunk. But does that make sense? I've never heard a person from Europe speaking their native tongue and thought, "Wow, he's sloshed." Not once has that thought occurred to me. It makes infinitely more sense to conclude that they were acting drunk because of the deep joy they were experiencing!

Holy Spirit drunkenness is just scratching the surface of this kind of manifestation. The Holy Spirit is also involved in deeply emotional encounters. Romans 8:26 says, "… for we do not know how to pray as we should, but the Spirit Himself intercedes for us with groanings too deep for words." The presence of the Spirit has led me into encounters where, in the same worship service, I was laughing in the Presence and sobbing as I prayed for the people of Iraq. It was the same Holy Spirit, but something about His presence can lead us into this sort of gut-wrenching travail. This sort of experience is not about setting up camp in negative emotions; it is about feeling grief over the suffering that befalls our brothers and sisters in the fallen world.

Encountering Jesus in a tangible way is a marking experience for anyone that has walked through it. Remember Saul in the book of Acts? In chapter 9, Saul had an encounter with Jesus that would change his life and the life of the church forever. Bright light flashed around Saul and he heard the voice of Jesus. The end result was he was left physically blind and he had to be led into the city by his companions. He would soon be healed by Jesus through Ananias, but the greater transformation was what took place on the inside. Saul was a new man, no longer a persecutor of Christians but a believer. It happened through an encounter with Jesus. I believe this is something like an accelerated renewing of the mind (Romans 12:2). Jesus can, through one touch, heal and renew the mind of a person.

I've had these sorts of encounters with Jesus. He really can bring freedom from addiction, heal old wounds of abuse and neglect, and correct lies we have believed in a single moment. His "one-step program" is incredible. It is almost like a touch from Jesus results in "rivers of living water" (John 7:38). These moments may be followed by a process of walking out the work that has taken place (such as Saul being led by his companions before he was healed through Ananias), but the truth is God's work can take place instantaneously.

We mustn't overlook the fact that an "overnight success" can take five years of preparation, lest we fail to celebrate the miracles that require long seasons of process beforehand. Whether it's an instantaneous move of God or a journey that leads to breakthrough, His goodness is steady at the helm.

On one occasion, while I was preparing to move from Green Bay to Redding, the physical labor of the move was beginning to overwhelm me somewhere between leaving home and uprooting my family on little more than a prophetic word. I was on the phone with a dear friend and prophetess named Belinda, who said to me, "Aaron, I see angels encamped all around you. You are leaving Egypt for the Promised Land." That word opened my eyes. When I focused on seeing, I actually saw the angels. Hundreds of them were gathered on our property. As I sat in total disbelief, from the far end of the property I saw the angels begin to bow down. Then, I saw Jesus walking toward me. I was so overwhelmed that I didn't know what to do next, so I sat down and stared. Jesus walked right up to me and put His arms around me. He whispered something in my ear and then left.

This experience was like lightning in my brain. (That's the only way I can adequately describe it.) I was sent into a spiral of intense revelation and healing that lasted for weeks. I don't recall how long I was laid out that day, but it ranks among the top prophetic experiences of my life. During that time period, I also heard the audible voice of God more often than ever before. It has always been a regular experience, but that touch from Jesus supercharged the gifts. I was hearing God speak daily, sometimes multiple times a day.

Remember, God wants to interact with His children even more than we want to meet with Him. His interaction can come in many forms, but there is a distinct manifestation of God beyond the indwelling of the Spirit and the omnipresence of the Deity. It is scriptural and it is beautiful. When God manifests in a particular way it is almost like heaven kisses earth. Believers are radically impacted, empowered, and transformed into a visage more like Christ than just moments earlier. It is a part of the Divine plan for individual growth and breakthrough.

THE IMPORTANCE OF DISCERNMENT

The seer is in an especially vulnerable role when it comes to their walk of faith, simply because of their constant interaction with the spiritual realm. I don't say this to scare anyone. Truthfully, a seer who is well grounded in their identity and under a spiritual covering can walk into a room and see demons cast out. I've seen this kind of deliverance many times. A person can develop a spiritual track record that makes demons shudder. More often, the seer will need to be intentional about including the Holy Spirit in processing visions and revelation than in identifying whether the manifestation before them is of God or of darkness. This is not to say that discernment is never needed when dealing with angels and demons. It's just a mistake to give undue credit to the enemy. Demons are easy to pick out. One verse about the devil coming as an angel of light (2 Corinthians 11:14) does not automatically ground a theology. Instead, let's focus on the overriding and ever-present fact that the devil is a defeated foe! At the cross Satan was defeated once and forever. His authority never belonged to him; it was always borrowed from the sons of man. Now, that authority belongs solely to Jesus, and He has given it freely to us!

Demons come to steal, kill, and destroy (John 10:10). If you are in the process of training your discernment (we all are on some level or another), start looking at the fruit of the spiritual partnership you make with your actions. Did you listen to instruction from an "angel" that gave you a creepy feeling? That angel may have been genuine. The book of Revelation alone tells us that not all angels are easy to understand. How many wings? Eyes?! But what was the fruit of partnering with that spiritual being? If you made a business decision and the business folded, that's destruction and theft. Many examples could be made, but the end point is to check the fruit when you are unsure. This will lead to a greater level of discernment. If an angel causes fear, that's fairly normal (Luke 2:10). If an angelic encounter leaves you with feelings of suicide, doubting your self-worth, or leaning toward sexual deviancy (pornography, etc.), ten to one you weren't having an encounter with an angel but a demon in disguise.

Revelation must also be guided by the Holy Spirit. I don't mean that revelation can sometimes come from the enemy, though a legitimate gift can be twisted by a familiar spirit. I'm referring to correctly interpreting the things God is genuinely showing you. For example, I recently had what I can only describe as one of the hardest nights of my life. Cally and I had gotten to bed later than we would have wanted, which isn't a rare occurrence in our house. I lay in bed for two or three hours seeing one vision after another, with cities on fire in every one of them. Now, I don't follow a gloom and doom prophetic philosophy and I've been in prophetic round tables where every word given for two hours straight was about God judging America and enemy tanks rolling across U.S. soil. God does warn of impending calamity, but it's because He is giving insight for His people to stand in the gap, as Abraham and Moses did, to mitigate a potential disaster.

These visions had my spirit troubled for the duration of the morning that followed, which just so happened to be a Sunday. I spent my entire drive to church re-playing the things I had seen the night before. I was actually beginning to decide that they had not been from God at all but were instead an attack from the enemy designed to discredit the authority of my own ministry and draw me into a place of mistrusting my gifts. I so disdain a prophetic focus that spreads fear and calls the goodness of God into question and was seriously in a rough spot. In my mind, there was no explanation aside from the thought that this was an obvious spiritual attack. Why else would I be up so late, and on a church night, no less?

Worship began, and it was simply glorious. There were angels all around and the presence of God was flowing through the room like waves of glory. Still, the only thing on my mind was the experience from the night before. Suddenly, the music was drowned out from my hearing by the voice of God, saying to me, "The fire is alive. Look again." I instantly saw clips of the visions from the night before. In each one the fire did not represent destruction and disaster but the presence of the Holy Spirit on cities and regions. What I had interpreted as destruction was actually a picture of revival sweeping across our land. God was actually giving me a glimpse of the very thing we had been praying for and laboring toward!

If we aren't careful, our expectation and worldview can limit our ability to function in any of the gifts. This is especially true when it comes to discernment and interpretation. For example, if you are accustomed to listening to prophetic voices who only speak negative and harsh words of correction, you will probably have a bent toward speaking the same sorts of words to overcome.

For the seer, there may have been voices saying that seers have to journey alone because of their unique gifts, or worse, that seers are especially vulnerable to demonic attacks. This can create a lens that stops a seer from being able to see the Kingdom side of the spiritual realm and sets them up for a string of bad experiences with the Church, simply because their worldview has been tainted by an expectation of rejection. The same way that my vision of revival was viewed through a lens of "the sky is falling" prophecy, any background static can make it hard to see what a vision is really trying to convey.

Discernment functions best in the context of community. 1 Corinthians 14:29 even suggests using discernment while prophetic words are being given. "Let two or three prophets speak, and let the others pass judgment." In this verse, the *prophecy* is judged, not the person giving the word. This is discernment in the confines of community! Relationship is a key to seeing the seer anointing grow and flourish, not just in experience, but in proper application. Learning to see a vision, dream, or glimpse of spiritual sight through the eyes and processing of others will help to create a more rounded interpretive method for the seer. This will never remove the need for community—far from it—but it will make quick discernment and interpretation on the fly come more naturally and accurately.

I once heard the story of a seer who saw what he interpreted to be a lifestyle of secret sin in another minster. He was then looking for an opportunity to confront the man, when the Holy Spirit brought him into a fierce revelation. The man wasn't engaging in sin but was merely being attacked by a demon that was trying to draw him into that behavior. The man was winning. Imagine how a confrontation with that man could have actually weakened his resolve, or brought an offense that could have opened the door to an even stronger demonic attack. That revelation allowed the seer to encourage and pray for the man rather than expose him for a sin he wasn't even guilty of committing!

On another occasion, I was taking my team along to pray through a home that had been the subject of a great deal of demonic activity. The goal was to train two gifted prophetic people (Becca and Justin) how to push back darkness in partnership with the Holy Spirit. A suicide had taken place in this home, and the man that had taken his own life was found by his grand-children. The spiritual atmosphere was a mess; the sort of place that makes the hair on the back of your neck stand up. After some prayer and a few prophetic acts (It may sound odd, but one of the team felt like they were supposed to act out "washing the walls in the Blood of Jesus," and it was powerful!), the atmosphere was totally shifted and redeemed.

As we were preparing to leave the homeowner asked if we could pray through his mother's home as well. She lived just down the street and had been seeing something in a specific area of her home for years. I had just gotten done training my team, so I stepped back and watched them do everything that we had just done to no avail. After asking questions of the homeowner and asking questions of the Holy Spirit they were coming up totally blank. She had been seeing a figure dressed in all white. There was no fear attached at all when she saw it, and though things in the house had been moved around, it didn't bother her. My interns came to me with blank faces; they just couldn't figure it out.

I had a pretty clear picture of what was going on by this point, but my job isn't always to answer questions. I asked about the fruit of the encounters and one of my team members blurted out, "well, it's not an angel!" Still, they were willing to entertain my wild notion. They started asking about specific objects that had been moved and the Holy Spirit started speaking almost instantly about the truth of this woman's identity that was being revealed through these objects. The Holy Spirit had been talking to her through an angel and she just didn't know how to hear Him.

Revelation is exciting, and seeing the heavenly realm is even more exhilarating. However, one must be careful not to let this excitement turn into brashness. Seeing something doesn't automatically mean you have a license to share. This is especially true if you're having a hard time sorting out the nature of what you saw. Sit on the experience and share it with other trusted prophetic people after the smoke has cleared. Getting community in on the process will help fine tune your gift and open doors to share even more vision and revelation in the future. This is especially true in a corporate setting. It cannot be emphasized enough; ask the Holy Spirit if you should share the things you are seeing! If you are having a hard time hearing His voice, ask a leader, trusted friend, or family member for help.

DEPLOYING THE SEERS INTO SOCIETY

Not all seers are called to be ministers (though all are called to the same Royal Priesthood). I know a few who would absolutely implode if they were put in charge of a congregation. Remember, a gift doesn't automatically qualify a person nor does it equal a call! There are just as many seers who are called to the business world as there are called to the church, and they have the opportunity to use their insight to make their leaders look like geniuses, bless the business, and advance the Kingdom.

I've almost always held an outside job in addition to doing ministry. It's only been in recent years that I have served in ministry in a full-time capacity. Disaster relief is a sphere that I will always have some connection with. It is simply wonderful to be able to carry hope into the midst of crisis and see people find stability in the midst of the hardest seasons of their lives.

A few years ago, the relief organization I was working with put on a Disaster Relief Training in Wisconsin. It was a prophetic swirl from start to finish, which often happens when the prophetic is part of an organization. It was truly beautiful: first aid, search and rescue, prophecy, healing, and deliverance all being trained under one roof. Our trainings were always designed with a specific scenario in mind. To make the training as much like a deployment as possible, the trainees would walk into a mock disaster and live "on-site" for three to five days, depending on the amount of material the training would cover. At the end, they would "graduate" and receive a certificate of completion.

For this training, I was tasked with writing the scenario. I simply sat down one day, not feeling particularly called or prophetic in my task, and jotted down a simple write-up. It said something like, "We are on the ground within seventy-two hours of a series of tornadoes devastating a small Midwest community. To exacerbate the relief efforts, within forty-eight hours of our arrival, a substation has caught fire, leaving much of the affected community without power."

On the last day of the training, we were in the final session when a lady's phone beeped in the back of the room. Missy, now a dear friend, was receiving a real-life storm alert message warning her to take shelter, as there was a tornado on the ground in her small, Midwest community. We responded immediately to this real-world incident after the training, which put us on the ground within seventy-two hours. Two days into the response, a substation caught fire and left part of the affected area without power.

It was like living in a dream as we helped people recover what was really important to them. God had protected this small community in that there was no loss of life, though we talked with families whose vehicles fell into the basement where they were hiding from the storm. Many people lost everything. The requests that we heard most often were for things like family photos, purses, and favorite stuffed animals that were lost amongst the debris. The chance of finding these things was pretty slim because of the nature of a tornado in a residential neighborhood. The streets that were once lined with well-manicured lawns and beautiful homes now looked like a giant landfill. Family photos from the area were found as far as sixty-five miles away. Remarkably, these were mostly undamaged though they had traveled a great distance exposed to the elements. What was even more remarkable was seeing the seer anointing in action on the site of a natural disaster.

I personally found toys, photos, purses, and other sought-after heirlooms and comfort items by tapping into this anointing. Just walking around the wreckage of a person's home with their "must-recover" items in my mind led to visual cues, visions, and spiritual sight that revealed the locations of these treasures. At one house, I was asking the Lord to reveal the location of a woman's purse that contained her ID, keys to her business, and other important items and family photos. It was then that I actually saw an angel pointing to a spot behind a fallen wall. Sure enough, the purse was right where the angel was directing me. The seer anointing is so valuable that it simply must escape the four walls of the church and be put to use in other arenas as well.

Teaching about the Seven Mountains or Seven Spheres of Influence has become very familiar in charismatic circles, so this is the vehicle that we will use to look at the role of the seer outside of the Church. This doesn't mean that the seer doesn't need the Church. Any such thought process is a trap. The mystical gifts are those most at risk if removed from the healthy boundaries and protection of community. Being in community, under a covering (not a legalistic control structure, but a system of strategic encouragement and empowerment), and in right relationship with teachers and people of discernment will safeguard the seer from wandering into an expression of faith that looks more like the New Age Movement than grounded, New Testament Christianity.

At the same time, I don't want to create a misconception that seers are superior to those with other gifts. If we, at any point, create a hierarchy that honors one gift over another we are moving away from the Kingdom. 1 Corinthians 12 makes it clear that the Body of Christ is made up of many different gifts, all of them equally valuable and relevant. This book, however, is focused on a very specific gift (the seer anointing) and to go outside of that scope would be detrimental to the effectiveness of our journey together.

THE SEER IN THE BUSINESS WORLD

The seer in the business world is well-positioned to make a tremendous impact for the Kingdom. I know it may not always seem this way on the surface, but the work of the Spirit is just as viable on the street as it is in the church. The business world is famous for being a "dog-eat-dog" environment. It is a place where keeping your head down and your weaknesses concealed will result in promotion and advancement, and keeping an inventory of the weaknesses and failures of the "competition" can give you the edge.

Imagine dropping a seer into this environment, specifically one who has tuned their gift to see the strength and the untapped gifts that lay dormant in the people around them. They walk through the office with a flashlight in one hand and a pick axe in the other, seeking to expose the *good* in people and shine their light on these things. They are a supernatural secret agent in the office, serving as a source of encouragement that strengthens the workforce and leads their co-workers into a revelation of their identity and destiny. They wage war against the kingdom of darkness in the midst of their daily responsibilities. When they see a demon taking shots at their boss, the demonic assignment is cancelled before it can be fulfilled as the seer partners with the Spirit to engage in spiritual warfare.

This is not a pipe dream; it is possible and even inevitable when a seer is fully alive, connected to the Spirit, and engaged in the life of an organization—even when it may not seem that what they are doing is very "spiritual." There is no line between sacred and secular; if you can do something in the church, you can do it anywhere. The only division is between our ears (in our minds). Even if your coworkers are unsaved, they will still benefit from being in an environment where demons have less available influence. The seer can make their workplace a safe place for people to escape torment that may be present in other areas of their lives.

As the seer uses their gift covertly, they find favor with the boss, who begins to ask their input on decisions. To those in the Church, the seer carries a profound prophetic gifting along with the seer anointing. To the boss, their intuition is usually right on and, before long, they have become something of a trusted advisor. Will they tell the boss that the reason they advised against the latest deal was because he saw darkness around the other company's rep? Probably not. Do they even need to do that? Again, probably not. But the end game is a lighter spiritual atmosphere in the office, which may eventually open doors to share the Gospel. This is amazing to think about! It is possible to have a business where the Spirit is allowed to breathe on prophetic gifts and encourage and edify a company of people to make their workplace and the greater community better.

The same is true in the small business world. Imagine a startup business based on the principles of the Kingdom and managed or owned by a seer! Not only do they offer a quality product, they have an opportunity to encourage and add strength to every person who walks through the door. I remember one particular night in Redding where my wife and I were just not connecting with one another in the way we normally would. When it came time to cook supper we realized that we had both thought the other person had pulled something out of the freezer. This didn't result in a fight, but a mutual sigh of defeat permeated the atmosphere.

We decided to pay a visit to Westside Pizza, a local spot just around the corner. When we entered, it seemed that the very atmosphere of the pizza shop washed our discouragement away. Before long, my wife and I were laughing and joking along with little Ren. The pizza wasn't that memorable. It was good, but it didn't exactly change my worldview on pizza. Still, this little shop had redeemed our evening. On the way out the door, Cally decided to stop and encourage the guy working behind the counter. She told them how our night had been going when we came in, how the atmosphere of the place seemed to immediately wash away our discouragement— and had even redeemed the time so we left with great joy.

His response was a bit shocking, as he boldly said, "I'm not surprised. It's because we worship Jesus in this place. When we're making food, running deliveries, or cleaning up, we're always praising Jesus." He continued to speak a prophetic word over our family! Westside Pizza became our go-to pizza place—not because they had the best pizza or the lowest prices—but because the presence of God had been cultivated in a way that made a tangible impact on the environment of what would otherwise be a normal pizza place.

People are drawn to the presence of God like moths to a flame. It's simply hardwired into our DNA. I wonder, sometimes, how many people were saved because they chose to buy a tent from the Apostle Paul. Remember, the clothes he would use to wipe his brow while working were sent off to heal the sick, along with pieces of his apron! (See Acts 19:12.) It's not hard to imagine that the people coming for Paul's services left with far more than they bargained for. If God can use a sweat rag to change the world, He can surely use a seer in the business world to work a miracle. We should expect this to happen! There is a God-encounter just waiting to happen every time someone walks into your shop. Every order, every item, every conversation is an opportunity to see the greatness in someone and call it forth.

THE ROLE OF THE SEER IN GOVERNMENT

The political system of this world has been the ire of the Church for as long as most of us can remember. We decry the lying, theft, and cronyism that seems to be hiding behind every corner. The truth is, things could be a lot better, but what are we doing aside from making nasty remarks and judgmental statements? When has shouting at the darkness ever produced the light we so desire?

We must stop partnering with the spirit of fatalism that is present in the political world and begin living out the Gospel. The seer is more than capable of doing this. The spirit of fatalism has so stormed our political system that it has almost become systemic. We use language like "the lesser of two evils" casually, as if this is a natural and normal occurrence and should be accepted as such. Imagine what might happen if a seer set foot on Capitol Hill with their mind set on being the hands and feet of Jesus, to serve the people who are bearing the brunt of the weight of leadership? Imagine what would happen if every leader had a Daniel in their court to see their potential instead of what they lack.

I believe seers are capable of developing strategic ways to impact both the spiritual and the physical realms when they are placed in positions of authority. For example, I vividly remember a ministry trip to New Orleans—the lower Ninth Ward, specifically. I've been all over the U.S. and even to the Middle East, and I've never encountered such an epidemic of the orphan spirit and poverty spirit as I did in Louisiana. They were everywhere we went. As a matter of fact, I'd imagine if you interviewed all of the persons in the neighborhood where we were ministering, the root of their physical issues would have been those two demonic forces, working in tandem, in nearly every individual. That is the spiritual root (superior reality) that leads to the physical manifestations we see in the Lower Ninth Ward. You cannot spend your way out of a poverty spirit, though that is the world's answer. Imagine if we applied what we know to this issue! Thankfully we were ministering with a team who understood the Greater Reality.

A seer in government is able to see to the root of the issue, far past the fruit that is so often seen as the sum total of the problem. For example, a city may see violence manifesting all around and racial tensions rising higher and higher—essentially a powder keg about to blow up. Their answer may be to train government workers to be fairer in dealing with people who are different than them. But the seer knows what is really taking place. These things are all fruit that stems from—let's say in this instance—a religious spirit of division and control that is keeping the people divided and focused on how their differences clash rather than the harmony that the Gospel provides. A strategy can then be formulated and carried out that strikes at the root of the problem and topples the plan of the enemy rather than a reaction that only sees the fruit and never deals with the underlying issue. Much of what we see in government today only deals with the fruit of a problem, when God desires to deal with the root!

The government and the nation could also stand to benefit greatly from some God-inspired legislation! This isn't to say that the Christian world wins by legislating morality in the nation. What I mean is we invite the Holy Spirit into an active role when drafting the laws of the land. There are Spirit-inspired answers to problems from budgets to crime prevention that lay undiscovered simply because no one has tapped into them. I long for the day when the public cries out for a solution to a problem—take energy for example—and the seer politician doesn't react with a press conference but responds by spending a block of time with Jesus to seek a solution. That seer then falls into a trance and has downloaded into their very mind and heart a solution born not of the logic of man but of the will of heaven. That day is just beyond the horizon!

Heaven has the answer to every crisis that currently faces man, and God has not hidden these things as a test, nor is He waiting for some super-Christian to attain a certain level of holiness that will loosen the lock on this revelation. It's encouraging to think that there must already be supernatural people in some of these positions. The U.S. alone has more than 500,000 elected officials between the federal, state, and local governments. As the seers begin to rise up and impact this sphere of society, we will see change brought forth.

Even if the seer doesn't hold a specific position in government, the opportunity to have influence is still clear. In the Old Testament, kings would almost always have prophets and seers in their court to aid in the decision-making process. Imagine the profound level of influence and opportunity that a seer could have as an advisor to the mayor, governor, or even the president! There are more people willing to hear the voice of God than we know, and these people are not limited to positions with little authority. Imagine King David's life without Samuel. In our lifetime, I believe we will have the opportunity to help shape the destiny of nations by influencing and advising the men and women who are in positions of influence. This is a holy task, to be sure.

THE SEER IN THE ARTS AND ENTERTAINMENT SECTOR

The world of the arts and entertainment seems almost tailor-made for the person who walks in the seer anointing. I honestly spent quite a few years of my life jealous of the people around me who had natural artistic abilities. They could paint, draw, sketch, and make the miracles of their imagination come to life. When I put pencil to paper, I actually had people wonder if my nonexistent children had made something for me (Cally and I had no children at the time). But imagine a seer with the ability to paint the glimpses they see of the spiritual realm. Imagine a poet able to put language to the activity of angels. It sends chills through my body just thinking about it!

We don't have to imagine, at least not entirely. There are two characters in our continuum of history who seem to fit into this mold rather nicely. One is William Blake, while the other Akiane Kramarik. William Blake (1757-1827) is something of an archetype of a seer in the world of art. According to many accounts, Blake began having open visions and spiritual sight occur on a regular basis very early in his life. Much of Blake's childhood was typical that of a young seer:

On another occasion, when he was eight or ten, sauntering along [on Peckham Rye, by Dulwich Hill], the boy looks up and sees a tree filled with angels, bright angelic wings bespangling every bough like stars. Returning home he relates the incident, and only through his mother's intercession escapes a thrashing from his honest father, for telling a lie. Another time, one summer morn, he sees the haymakers at work, and amid them angelic figures walking (Bentley 1969, 542-543 cited in Bentley 1975, 36-37).

Blake also interacted with the angelic realm in a way that is common for many seers. On one occasion:

I was one day reading Young's *Night Thoughts,* and when I came to that passage which asks "who can paint an angel," I closed the book and cried, "Aye! Who can paint an angel?" A voice in the room answered, "Michael Angelo could." "And how do *you* know," I said, looking round me, but I saw nothing save a greater light than usual. "I *know*" said the voice, "for I sat to him: I am the arch-angel Gabriel." "Oho!" I answered, "you are, are you: I must have better assurance than that of a wandering voice; you may be an evil spirit- there are such in the land." "You shall have good assurance," said the voice, "can an evil spirit do this?" I looked whence the voice came, and was then aware of a shining shape, with bright wings, who diffused much light. As I looked, the shape dilated more and more; he ascended into heaven; he stood in the sun, and beckoning to me, moved the universe (Bentley 1975, 37).

In adulthood many thought him mad, though Blake had probably just gone the way of a number of seers who possess little understanding of their gift nor belong to a community that keeps them grounded in truth. Blake continued in visions, spiritual sight, and other experiences until his death.

Akiane Kramarik is a well-known child prodigy and painter of *Prince of Peace* and countless other masterpieces. What you may not know is that she began having visions and seeing into the spiritual realm at the young age of four. She was driven to express the wonders that she was experiencing through whatever artistic medium was close at hand (WSInt 2014). This certainly sounds like a textbook activation of the seer anointing. Her parents, who were atheists, even came to faith in Christ after she began having these incredible encounters! Today, Akiane is a household name—or her art is at least recognizable by many people. Even if you haven't heard her name, there is a good chance you have seen her work. Akiane has had an opportunity to impact culture in a spectacular way without compromising or hiding who she is and what she carries.

There are more out there, and I suspect that many of the masters of antiquity carried a similar gift. This goes beyond the world of pen and brush. We are living in a world that is marching to the beat of an entertainment-driven society in ever-increasing degrees. For too long we have turned our back or searched for a way to "Christianize" secular entertainment. A good friend of mine refers to this as the "Christian Ghetto" mindset and I cannot fault him in the reasoning. I've seen movies that I saw as a child remade in an attempt to reach a new generation. Stories told over and over because it seems Hollywood is running dry on ideas. It's almost like the whole machine is perishing due to a lack of revelation, which is interesting since we as believers have the market near cornered on fresh revelation and, for the most part, have turned our backs on Hollywood.

What would it look like if the inspiration for a summer blockbuster came from an open vision? How could society be impacted and influenced if we saw the opportunity to express heaven and the love of Jesus through the media that is most readily encountered and consumed by the generations at large? The future of the Church doesn't just exist in internet broadcasts and slick digital design, it exists in expressions of our values and our experience with Jesus that don't just leak out of the context of the church building, but are purposefully built to be experienced along with other mainline forms of entertainment. I can guarantee that some of the people reading this very line have had a vision or seen something play out in their mind, or even seen something happen in the spirit and thought, "This would make an awesome movie, story, television show, etc." The Holy Spirit may well have dropped a tool for impacting our world into your lap!

Stories hold universal impact and significance. The prophetic realm is ripe with inspiration for stories to be told. Not corny Christian takes on classic tropes with built in "Jesus Moments," but real and authentic tales spun with excellence and designed to draw the audience into an encounter with the great I AM.

THE SEER IN EDUCATION

Whether we want to admit it or not, educators hold more sway for the development of the average child than most people they will encounter. Even more than parents in some circumstances. This influence is growing at an exponential rate, with the university system perhaps doing just as much as primary schools to shape the worldview of our young people. This may come as a shock, but not all educators have a Kingdom worldview! In my own life, I have had teachers who left me with baggage (the belief that I wasn't as intelligent as other children because I couldn't sit still, for example). This is not to put down teaching as a profession, but to show that there needs to be a shift in the way that some teachers interact with students.

Enter the seer. They can speak out what they see on a student's life in a way that goes beyond mere "encouragement." In our ministry, we had seasons where teens just seemed to be drawn to our little church for no natural reason. We took those opportunities very seriously. Some of these kids were already parents, and some were so starved for love and acceptance that just thinking of them breaks my heart. We took advantage of every opportunity to speak life into them. There were times when I would speak a sneaky prophetic word over one of them, and I say "sneaky" because I would basically tell them what I saw on and around them in non-religious terms, to later find out I was the first person to call something like that out of them in their entire lives. Cally and I had the honor and privilege to be the first to see their potential and get a glimpse of their destinies. But how heartbreaking it is to go that long without anyone seeing any potential in you.

The educational system is filled with these types of students, and their numbers are growing at an increasingly alarming rate. They are brilliant, gifted, called, and they carry the spark of destiny inside them. At the same time, they come from broken homes, many are fatherless, and before they are old enough to drive a car they carry crippling wounds that need to be healed.

I have a deep desire to see the Church rise up and use our gifts to give these would-be world changers a fighting chance! In the same way that a seer in the sphere of government can see the root of a problem, so can a seer in the educational system.

I myself was a troubled kid to say the least. My dad left when I was six months old (we reconnected years ago, and God did wonders in fully restoring that relationship). That, and a hundred other factors turned me into an angry kid. It took years in the education system to find that one teacher who would call out the gold in me instead of pointing out the dirt, as so many teachers before him had done. It wasn't a profound prophetic word that changed my life, but a simple encouragement that might have been a standard way to encourage troubled kids. He told me that I was a leader and that people were watching, that my behavior meant something. His words were life to my aching heart. I was still a troublemaker, but something about that little dose of encouragement brought something inside of me to life that is still alive to this day. Without those words, I doubt I would still be alive today, let alone a leader in my spheres of influence.

If a word like that can change a person's life, a prophetic word—let alone a vision—can go much deeper, in a way that is hard to fathom. You have the power, influence, and authority to send a word like this right into the spirit of the person in front of you, whoever they may be. It doesn't undo the hurts and the pain that they may be carrying, but it's a start. During the early years of their development, a seer could have a ridiculous level of impact. Call out the gold in those children. Do it at every opportunity that presents itself, especially in traditional disciplinary situations. With the proper motivation and maneuvering, it might be possible to start a ripple effect of encouragement among the rest of the kids in their class.

In the university setting the seer is no less able to elicit change. This is another formative period for every individual who chooses to pursue higher education. In this time specifically dedicated to training and preparation for a lifelong career, a generation is susceptible to the ebb and flow of ideas in academia. This isn't lost on the enemy, and the world of higher education has become more hostile toward the Gospel in the last few decades than ever before. This has resulted in a machine that appears as though it was purposefully designed to churn out atheists and agnostics.

There is hope in seers and prophetic people taking up residence in these settings. Not only can they speak words of life into a generation, they can discern the root of the darkness that is moving on campus and work to push it back so the Kingdom of heaven may be unleashed. What is strange is that the "spirit of the age" in the academic community appears to be rooted in the religious spirit. Now, hear me out. We see a system where freedom of thought is taught, but in practice only a few approved systems are actually lauded and allowed without persecution. Control is applied both overtly and covertly to keep students in line. There are even a number of long dead adherents to the "faith" that are venerated in the cathedral of the learned (Freud comes to mind). This sounds like a few churches I know, and it definitely sounds like a secular college experience!

As seers rise up to combat the undertow that is taking place in our schools and universities, they have a very real chance to stymie the tide. Prayer, spiritual warfare, speaking positivity into the lives of students and staff, and simply carrying the Presence of God into the educational setting are all strategies that give Jesus a beautiful opportunity to move.

THE SEER IN THE MEDIA

The media world is under attack in a way that is hard to fathom. This attack isn't just coming from the realm of darkness, it's also coming from the Church! Life and death are in the power of the tongue (Proverbs 18:21), and we have done a poor job of releasing life over the media with the words we speak. How often do you hear rants about the "secular media," the "liberal media," and their negative impact on our society? When a royal, prophetic priesthood (1 Peter 2:9) allows these sorts of things to be constantly on our lips, it's no wonder that things have actually begun to look as bad as we have claimed!

There is another answer, without a doubt. It starts with recognizing the impact that the media world has, but doing so in a positive and hopeful way—through the eyes of the King. Seers can recognize the disparity between the good that they see in the world and the negativity that the current media machine is pumping out 24/7. This disparity is linked, I believe, to a dominant spirit of fatalism that has been infiltrating the marketplace and the Church for longer than we'd like to admit. One of my spiritual fathers often says, "You better believe that the news media is prophetic. They prophesy every evening—some 24/7—and it changes the nation."

A friend of our family who lives in Redding once had a whimsical idea. What would it be like to produce news that was positive at heart instead of leaving the positive stories as an afterthought to the day's "real" news? If we truly believe that what we consume will have an influence on our minds and spirits, we must be mindful of our media consumption, but also seek to improve the quality of available media.

A Kingdom-focused media outlet would be the most amazing answer to this issue. However, this is likely not feasible, and a reinforcement of the aforementioned "Christian Ghetto."(There are several Christian news outlets in existence, but these can often be just as negative as the secular stations and not an accurate reflection of the Kingdom.) What we really need is to revamp the media world at every level by bringing seers into this sphere of influence, as they carry a vivid vision of the future where the defeated foes of sin and death are on the run from a victorious Bride and the secular world has bowed its knee to the King of Kings. A vision of the enemies of Christ made His footstool. This sort of positivity can change the atmosphere of a state, nation, and even an entire planet, whereas our focus on negativity has gotten us nowhere.

It seems that mass shootings have been on the rise in the U.S. in recent years. I'm not going to comment on political policy, mostly because this isn't a policy issue; it's an issue of focus. When a deranged and demonized soul wreaks havoc on those around him, the media floods our imaginations with accounts, video feeds, pictures of the madman, etc. This continues for weeks, and I believe this excessive focus draws the next madman out of the woodwork. Before we know it, the cycle continues. What would happen if this sort of tragedy was given thirty seconds of airtime, and the only mention was focused on prayer and support for the victims with little glorification of the perpetrator? What would happen if the mass media made such a dramatic shift that miracles of healing and accurate prophetic words became newsworthy?

A host of seers, calling out the good and the greatness in our leaders, and highlighting the effect of ministry, helps projects, and good old-fashioned human decency can shift our focus to the opposite end of the spectrum. I cannot wait to see a newscast that details a revival atmosphere striking a church in the United States. I cannot wait to see a news anchor speak a prophetic word or make a prophetic declaration from their position of influence!

Breaking news could be even more breaking for the seer. I've heard a number of accounts of members of law enforcement on the hunt for a certain person, using their prophetic gifting to find a dangerous subject after the trail had gone cold. This sort of insight, I imagine, is already at play for many members of the media. Investigative journalism would be taken to a whole new level if the journalist were led by the Holy Spirit. It is impossible to overestimate the good that could be done and the evil that could be undone. God can and will raise up people to confront evil, just as He always has. Whether seers are serving these people or they actually are those that hear the call, the value of these gifts is a dramatic advantage.

We must also realize that the leaders in media have a great deal of influence over which stories get traction and which seem to fall by the wayside of history. This is why we need to have Kingdom-minded people in the higher levels of the media world. This sounds like classic dominionism, and it is to an extent. I would reject the "by any means necessary" vernacular, but the call to these positions is out there among us. If God has called you, your call is valid! A close friend of mine received a prophetic word along the lines of "you will become the most powerful man in media." This sounds like a strange and specific word, unless we have realized the importance of blurring the imaginary line between the sacred and secular and, more importantly, taken a cue from biblical history and seen what tremendous good can be carried out by a Kingdom representative in a position of power and influence. Just as Joseph became the most powerful man in Pharaoh's kingdom and used his position to save his people, a man or woman in this position can devastate the enemy and promote Jesus to an entire culture.

THE SEER AT HOME

The family unit is the most important building block of society. To destroy the family unit is to destroy a nation. The opposite is also true. No matter how far a people has fallen, there is hope if the family unit can be restored to a place of health and prominence.

Ministry begins at home. Before any of us can have impact on the dynamics of families in our region, our families must first be healthy. One of my personal mantras has been "Family never goes on the altar." I've watched many families implode because ministry became "more important." Your children receive the first fruits of your ministry, no question. If I have a revelation, it goes to my family before it ever goes to the church or the community. The same is true of my time. I've told my church and ministry school that they get the leftovers, the overflow, of what God is doing in my family. Anything less is outside the will of the One that chose to call Himself "Father." Ministry is service to God, but it is *not* God in itself. Confusion in this area is a setup for burnout and failure. It's difficult to help others create healthy family when you don't have a healthy family!

Seers are often equipped to see the dynamics of a family in their sphere. This isn't a license to step in and correct things that are out of line, but an opportunity to call out the health in a family that may be buried under misunderstanding, grief, and years of eroded connection. Seeing the family as God sees it and declaring that heavenly reality is often the connecting point for God to bring restoration.

Our church has partnered with a ministry called Life Skills that has been doing amazing marriage and family work for years. Their heart to see people step into their identity in all areas of life is breathtaking. I believe one of the things that makes them so effective is they have caught a glimpse of God's vision for the family and for healthy marriages. They see what is possible and are able to not only equip people to walk it out, but speak transforming, healing truth from the heart of Jesus.

The seer is also well-suited for the realm of social work. I have a great deal of respect for social workers in every sphere. Their dedication to the wellbeing of people reflects the heart of the Father. Imagine a seer called to either support or take part in social work that involves dysfunctional families and at-risk youth. Who better to untangle the web of addiction, behavioral crisis, and illness that plagues so many than one who can see God's heart for a family and strategically tear down the spiritual strongholds that bear physical [negative] fruit in the family? Who better than the seer to speak words of life and destiny over the young person who has been told by their peers, family, and society that they aren't valuable and have nothing to contribute?

The family unit will be healed when we are willing to stop only speaking out against the darkness and begin acting to change it. We were created to shine as lights in a darkened world. It all starts with one person making an impact in their sphere of influence. It may not seem like much by itself, but it can create a ripple effect that makes a dramatic shift in an arena. There are people all around you—even in your church—who desperately need what God has put inside of you. They need your wisdom, experience, and positive influence. There are families on the brink of destruction, marriages that walk the tightrope each and every day. Take holy responsibility and adopt a family to mentor, encourage, and equip. It could be the start of a movement that breaks the cycle in families across an entire region!

THE SEER IN RELIGION

The religious sphere holds a dear place in my heart for a number of reasons. The greatest of which is probably my years of pastoral ministry, beginning with the church my wife and I planted as teenagers. (Yes, we were only eighteen!) However, I also fell out of love with the Church after ten years of difficult ministry. If it were not for the season we spent at Bethel, my family would have succumbed to ministry burnout and been among the walking wounded instead of sprinting and growing in a place of victory.

Now that I have been off of the battlefield long enough to convalesce, I can honestly say I have fallen back in love with the Church—in all of her expressions and with all of her quirks. I have also never felt as alive and at home doing ministry as I do in this season of life. It helps to find a ministry that embraces the gifts and call on your life, or at least to be in a place where the gifts of the Spirit—even the less understood ones—are welcome and are being actively sought out. There is something about being under the covering of healthy leadership that makes ministry come alive.

The seer should be at home in the Church. It is our home in a very real way. A healthy church will have more angelic activity, and, strangely enough, more demonic activity than almost anywhere else. There is something about the presence of Jesus that draws people in to either use their gifts or get free of oppression. In that sort of environment, the seer is in their element. This shouldn't be too shocking. Any precursory study of our heritage will show people with the seer anointing coming out of the woodwork. Most of the saints that history remembers as mystics were probably seers. The Church attracts those with these gifts, simple as that.

As we have concluded, not all seers are called to vocational ministry, but one would be hard-pressed to find a ministry situation that would not benefit from a seer's presence and expertise. From discerning the seasons for sermon series to back-room deliverance, the seer is a valuable resource. Even if the church's leadership isn't heavy laden with seers, the gift can be pulled on by the people in leadership. In the same way that Samuel was a trusted advisor to the king, a seer can serve in an advisory role to the leadership of a church. I think this is a key to victory in the next season. Not only must churches become seer-friendly, they must make room for seers in the decision-making and course-setting for the ministry.

This doesn't mean seers get to steer the ship from the back, but it would be a failure to think that their gift isn't important enough to give it a voice. My first experience with our home church was attending my second service and seeing something between an open vision and spiritual sight over the ministry. I struggled a bit with what to do with it, then decided to approach the pastor and share what I had seen. I was terribly blunt with him. "I know that I don't know you from Adam, but I saw something during worship; is it okay if I share it with you so you can decide what to do with it?"

He granted me permission and I shared the full detail of my experience. I quickly sensed that it was troubling to him. He didn't react externally, and I found out after the fact that his response to what I shared was to gather other prophetic people and ask them to judge what I had told him. They confirmed it was a spot-on word from God. The pastor and his wife spent the rest of the week praying into what God had shown them.

The following Sunday before the service began, the pastor made a beeline for me. He embraced me and thanked me for having the courage to share what the Lord had shown me. During the service, he publicly acknowledged me and shared the vision and the response of the leadership with the entire congregation!

With a little focused attention, this became less rare of an occurrence. Even if a seer is called to vocational ministry, the combination of their gift and the freedom to be an individual in the body is powerful and magnetic. The Church is hungry for the supernatural! The word of God never returns void and its preaching is never to no effect, but when a church aligns itself in the direction that God is moving the effects can be radically multiplied. Like any expression of the prophetic, the seer can be a tremendous part of the sail that catches the wind of where God's Spirit is blowing and cause the church to move forward. Changes that would normally takes months or years in our own strength can happen in days and weeks when the Spirit is moving. Seers can help us to know *when* and *how* this is taking place.

CHAPTER 6

THE SEER ANOINTING AND OTHER PROPHETIC GIFTS

Like all spiritual gifts, the seer anointing functions best in community and must also come alongside the other gifts in order to create a robust prophetic culture. I have noticed the seer anointing seems to flow in a similar manner as the feeler/mercy gift. Feelers tend to have an emotional empathy that allows them to pick up on what's happening in the spiritual realm through their emotions. I suppose it would make sense to call this emotional processing, wouldn't it? The seer sees and the feeler feels. I know a pastor who is a feeler, and he will talk about how it often seems like I see the same thing that he feels in a setting.

My wife is also a feeler, one with a measure of anointing I rarely encounter. We were talking about the supernatural one night when I blurted out, "That dark-winged angel is awesome!"

I had just returned from a missions trip to New Orleans, and I noticed right away that the angel that I'd grown accustomed to seeing wasn't anywhere to be seen! I was trying to figure this out during one of the many briefings of the trip.

I had just finished telling Cally about being in New Orleans and losing track of that particular angel. I thought maybe he'd stayed home to watch over Cally and Ren or something. In my wondering, movement out of the corner of my eye caught my attention. I looked up to see the angel dragging a small demon down the hallway of the missions base by the scruff of its neck. When I finished the story, Cally stopped me.

"Did you feel that?" she asked. I had felt a tiny shift in the atmosphere, but it wasn't significant enough for me to really take note of. She looked over at me and continued, "I think they like it when we get excited about what they're doing; it felt like joy was dumped into the atmosphere."

Since then, I've been far more intentional about bragging on the angels that hang around our family! Perhaps the prophetic person can even edify and encourage angels. They do the work of heaven for the benefit of the saints. It makes sense that we would brag on them!

It is also possible to partner with the Holy Spirit in healing. I've watched people get healed in the spiritual realm as they were healed in the physical realm. It was a little strange the first time, but it has happened enough times since for me to take notice. A dear friend from our church had injured her shoulder at work and was about to have surgery. We brought her to a home group with us, where we felt a strong sense that Jesus wanted to heal the sick. One of the leaders prayed over her shoulder, and while he was praying I saw what looked like an x-ray of the whole joint with a bright light tracing and outlining different structures.

The woman was healed! I've seen similar things since, and any time this particular vision has come to me, the person receiving prayer has been healed.

Another thing to note is seers will often be affected by happenings in the spiritual realm that impact other prophetic types. One of the constant themes I heard at Bethel was the idea that supernatural encounters always increased when a conference was about to take place at the church. It made sense to me, but I wasn't sure how it would play out in reality. I paid close attention during the next conference, and I watched my daughter as well.

A few days before, it became very difficult to get Ren to sleep at night. This was out of character for her, though she had gone through similar phases in the past. My wife then saw the moms' Facebook group she was a part of light up. Every parent she knew in the community was having the *exact* same problem. That night, I decided I would experiment with my gift a bit and see just what was going on. I ended up seeing demons—many more than I typically see in a week—in one night. They were actually walking around the outside perimeter of our apartment, as if they were trying to find a way inside. Apparently, they were correct about an increase in supernatural activity!

Analogy is the easiest way I have found to explain the Kingdom, as it is so vast (and, honestly, so good) that stories and word pictures seem to be the best avenue to get through to people. I often picture it as a battlefield with every person doing their part. The prophetic realm is like a communication and observation outpost. Messages from headquarters (heaven) are constantly coming in and being relayed to the troops. The prophetic people also keep an eye on the enemy, which the seers can do literally! Seeing enemy troop movement in advance can make a huge difference in the battle. The traps the devil tries to lay for us are easily undone and cast down when we can see them. With seers in the mix, this is easily accomplished. If we understand our identity in Christ and know what the enemy is plotting, we become an unstoppable force.

A SUPERNATURAL AWAKENING

Part of why the seer anointing is so important in this season has to do with a mass supernatural awakening taking place around the world, which is not happening in the Church alone. The obsession with all things spiritual seems to be growing faster in secular culture than it's growing in Church culture. The only difference is we aren't chasing after counterfeits, but focusing on real and authentic expressions and manifestations of Jesus.

The seer gets to bring people into the wonder-filled world of their experience. They are the open door to the supernatural realm that people desperately hunger for. This growing hunger has created a desire to operate in the seer anointing, which means more and more people are stepping into the gift and stepping out to admit that they already walk in it!

The charismatic movement is in no way new, but as Church culture becomes more and more prophetic, the pull on the seer anointing will only increase. A seer can do much in this setting to aid in the creation and sustaining of a healthy prophetic culture. I say "healthy" because prophetic culture is still a fairly new thing to many churches. Because the seer anointing is very visible in many ways, mismanagement from any angle can lead to either the seer running the show or building a sub-ministry that takes away from what God is doing in the corporate setting. The opposite can be just as detrimental. A seer who finds no outlet to use their gift will either stop using it or go rogue, just for the opportunity to fully express who they are in the Kingdom.

Neither of these are the correct path. What we need is, once again, a healthy prophetic culture. We must raise up spiritual mothers and fathers who will pour into the next generation, train them to walk in the gifts God has given them, and allow them to step into leadership opportunities. Every church has people who walk in the supernatural and are dying to connect with others who have had similar experiences. A young seer who I've been spending time with in Green Bay, WI told me he had been praying for a mentor in the gift to come along for over a year. That's just the period of time that he recognized the need for mentorship. I could have used one for the last thirty years! I'm not bitter because I know God wastes nothing and without that time in the wilderness I wouldn't have come into the place of peace and expectancy I've discovered. Perhaps the breakthrough that so many seers are stepping into right now can be a propelling point for the next generation of seers and mystics as they take their place among us.

Why are people waiting half of their lives to encounter Jesus the way that some seers and mystics do on a regular basis? This is a question that has haunted me for years. Any time I've heard someone talk about wanting to actually see the Lord, or heard someone talk about that one supernatural experience that they had in their youth that has driven them onward into the Kingdom, it stirs something deep inside of me and I hope it does for you as well.

Imagine a child growing up without a father, as I did. Dad either left at an early age for this little one, or he wasn't there from the start. But there are a few pictures and a letter that he wrote. This letter has become that little girl's tear-stained prize. She reads it, re-reads it, hoping that one day she will get to see her daddy again, or worse, for the first time. Every word is important to her, every line. She waits by the phone, hoping he will call. She checks the mail every day, hoping for a letter from him. Nothing ever comes. We wouldn't exactly be lining up to give this dad an award, would we?

We've done this with our understanding of God! He left us the Bible; we read it, re-read it, hoping we will get to meet Him one day. To make matters worse, the letter He left us with continuously talks about Him spending time with His other children! Perhaps He loves us a little less, or we just haven't been good enough. Maybe He only visited His children for a really brief period of history and He is no longer doing so. Or maybe, just maybe, we are wrong about who He is and His desire to interact with us. A father who fails to interact with His kids is neglectful. A God who does the same is not worth following.

The good news is God is not like that! The New Testament call, "Repent, for the kingdom of heaven is at hand" literally means, "Adjust your thinking, because God is here!" As the supernatural expressions of the Kingdom grow, we will not be able to keep the hungry ones out of the church. We could put a moat full of crocodiles and piranhas around the place and they would find their way in. It's already like this for the seers. In the last few years, the number of people in the Church who walk in this anointing has increased exponentially. It's almost as though God is gathering them in preparation for a breakthrough that is on the horizon.

This breakthrough has been in the building stages for far longer than our collective lifetimes. Remember, God is a long game player. What if He has been sowing the seeds of the next Great Awakening for generations? What if we've been looking at the spiritual positioning of the nations all wrong? What if every negative prophetic word we've heard over the last fifty years was merely the result of a prophetic culture filtering the hope of the coming Kingdom through an Old Covenant lens?

As a side note, revival doesn't just happen by the ebb and flow of the sovereignty of God, nor is it a critical mass of prophetic words over a region. Revival is, in my opinion, a holy moment when a personal revelation becomes a corporate revelation. *I am revival.* When this reality catches on, it becomes a wildfire that cannot be contained. We have seen revival ushered in by intense conviction over sin. We have seen revival sparked by a fresh revelation of the goodness of the Father. We have even seen waves of revival overtake our land in the wake of the power of Jesus made manifest in a band of California hippies! That is proof enough that it doesn't take perfect people to see the Kingdom advance.

The next wave of revival will be carried by a hunger for the supernatural. God has been drawing the nations, especially America, toward this hunger for a purpose. Imagine how much greater our impact would be if we honored the hunger and openness of the spiritualists, new agers, and wiccans rather than condemning every part of what they do! Do I agree with their beliefs and practices? Absolutely not. But I know that God has given them a hunger and, often times, a genuine spiritual gift [expressed the wrong way]. They can be grafted in. This doesn't mean they get to slap "Christian" on their old way of life. Honor their hunger and show them a better way. Much of their experience is a paltry counterfeit to our authentic experience. I've met prophets, mystics, and seers who came to the Church to find a safe place to express their gifts. What they found was a religious system that didn't have room for them. If we make room for them, we will win them back. Moreover, we will see a missing dimension of the Church return, which cannot help but fan the flames of revival that are already smoldering.

Those outside the Body have an excuse. No one has taught them that their gifts are valuable, biblical, or important for the advancement of the Gospel and the Kingdom. This makes sense at the base level. Seers and prophets won't make an impact if they don't know what they carry. But what about those inside of the Church? What is their excuse?

FALSE HUMILITY

C.S. Lewis (who I consider to be a spiritual father of mine due to the impact of his writings) wrote of his view on humility in *The Screwtape Letters*. According to Lewis, humility isn't so much about taking a low view of yourself as it is placing your focus on the wellbeing of others. Here, he writes from the enemy's point of view:

"You must therefore conceal from the patient the true end of Humility. Let him think of it not as self-forgetfulness but as a certain kind of opinion (namely, a low opinion) of his own talents and character. Some talents, I gather, he really has. Fix in his mind the idea that humility consists in trying to believe those talents to be less valuable than he believes them to be ... By this method thousands of humans have been brought to think that humility means pretty women trying to believe they are ugly and clever men trying to believe they are fools. And since what they are trying to believe may, in some cases, be manifest nonsense, they cannot succeed in believing it and we have the chance of keeping their minds endlessly revolving on themselves in an effort to achieve the impossible. To anticipate the Enemy's *(God's)* strategy, we must consider His aims. The Enemy wants to bring the man to a state of mind in which he could design the best cathedral in the world, and know it to be the best, and rejoice in the, fact, without being any more (or less) or otherwise" (Lewis 2001, 70-71, italics added).

This sort of false humility is the plague of the seer. To put it plainly, visions need to be shared. There is nothing humble about sitting on revelation because you don't feel worthy to take a place in the spotlight. Seers weren't born to be glory hounds and those addicted to attention but that doesn't mean we should keep incredible revelations quiet because we don't want to draw attention to ourselves. (This applies to far more than just seers, but I don't know that I've talked with a single seer in my lifetime who didn't struggle with this at one point.) The enemy loves to bring fear into a person's life; it's his greatest strategy. Whether it's fear of being seen as crazy, fear of speaking in public, or any other number of fears, the devil will use it to keep seers silent. Now, this doesn't mean every experience needs to be shared.

It doesn't mean the seer should violate covenant with leadership to speak out a "burning word." It means that the Holy Spirit is still the ultimate guide for effective use of the gift, and gifts are always used in covenant and in honor.

I recently had a run in with fear while integrating into a new church, something I hadn't done in ten years. The leadership of this church had cleared me to give prophetic words in the confines of their protocol. The fear that came up had to do with sharing experiences too often. I found myself asking my wife how often it would be appropriate to share things I had seen. Is there a socially acceptable number of prophecies before you begin violating the culture of the church? What I was really hearing was the enemy whisper in a familiar old voice of false humility.

Who am I? is probably a question we ask far too often. Earlier, I recounted the time I had heard a leader in the faith talk about the few times they had experienced the audible voice of God. That was a "who am I?" moment for me. I felt a sense of unworthiness in the frequency with which I'd had these experiences. False humility is more interested in *your* identity than God's, and it is radically unhealthy. This voice is a killer and a thief masquerading as honor.

Seers are brought down by this lying voice. It claims that every word is a cry for attention, every vision shared is showing off, and every testimony is a brag. We must not listen to this voice! God is pouring out revelation all the time, twenty-four seven, yet we often allow the enemy to dictate what can and cannot be released. That is crazy! There is nothing humble about thinking we aren't good enough, righteous enough, or eloquent enough to share what God is doing.

False humility will also attempt to take the mystic down with a vicious cycle of defeat and despair. The seer is drawn to a person who they think simply needs an encouraging word and they wind up giving them a whopper of a prophetic word instead. The enemy then begins to plant seeds of doubts in the seer's mind in an attempt to cause them to pass up opportunities to share what they are seeing. Being the liar he is, he begins to whisper things along the lines of, "You really blew it" and "Now that person isn't going to get healed." Sound familiar? For many seers, it is.

We must combat the lies of the enemy and reclaim our voice. This process is daunting and it can involve tremendous risk depending on our environment, but it must be done. There is no way around it. False humility is the bane of the supernatural realm. Imagine if the Gospel writers had decided not to write because they were too afraid of drawing attention to themselves. Look at the Gospel of John, the only Gospel that calls the Apostle John "The one Jesus loved" (John 13:23, among other places). We would roast a guy for doing that today, but no one is lining up to call John proud or arrogant. John simply understood who he was.

We must have the same understanding. Seers are gifted for a reason. It's not just a fun thing we do for our own amusement. Every gift seems to have both a personal and corporate significance. Meaning seers see into the Spirit, not just for their own good, but for the good of those around them. We squash the latter and greater of those two realities when we shut our mouths out of fear of what others will think of us, which is really just the fear of man.

The other side of the coin is the release of Kingdom when we are willing to share our experience. It is nothing short of miraculous to see God work through the experience of just one person. There is freedom in owning your gift. Truly owning it, accepting the label of "seer," the whole shebang. People will start asking questions like, "What do you see on me?" and "Are there any angels around me? What do they look like?" This is good! It means they are hungry for the things of God. The pressure they put on you to use your gift is a beautiful kind of pressure (though it does not mean it is your inescapable responsibility to see something for them). It's the sort of squeezing that leads others to step into the gift or come forward and admit that they too walk in the seer anointing.

There is nothing humble about pretending you are small and insignificant, or your gifts don't exist. There is also nothing humble about disavowing your destiny. In fact, when a gifted person refuses to walk in their gift it grieves the heart of God! If God is a good Father, it's hard to imagine Him enjoying it when we put ourselves down and go out of our way to pretend we are worth so little. I believe this is more rooted in the fear of man than it is a desire to please God.

The time has come to stop fearing man. Condemnation doesn't come from the Kingdom. It just doesn't. Anything that reduces who you are in Christ is a lie from the enemy. False humility is a sin because it takes a gift that deserves to be put on display to bring God glory and hides it. It's like taking a Picasso painting and putting it in the basement under an old blanket. Sure, it's safe, but it's not bringing the enjoyment and inspiration that it was intended to bring.

COMING OUT OF THE WILDERNESS

Seers are a rare breed, but they are becoming more and more common—especially as people who have previously hidden their gift find the freedom to walk in it. I remember the process of coming to grips with the role my gifts played in shaping my identity. It all started when a dear old friend of mine named Joe pulled me aside after I had the opportunity to play a role in a remarkable church service. I was on a spiritual high after such an evening, but there was something that Joe wanted to address. He went on to tell me that the reason why God had showed up to the extent that He did during the service was because, as he put it, "You were being you." He went on to give me permission to be myself from the pulpit from that moment forward.

Becoming "myself" was a gradual process, one that began by allowing more of my personality to come through when I preached, with less filtering based on what I thought a "pastor" should be! From a Five-fold ministry perspective, I'm not a pastor. That's part of why it was so difficult. I was trying to pastor people (care for their needs with love and connection) rather than call them to their destiny and equip them to hear the voice of God. Simply put, being a pastor was draining me because I am not wired to be that sort of pastor.

Slowly, I began sharing bits and pieces of a history with God that had been kept secret for decades. The church was pretty understanding, but nobody had really seen the things I had seen. This was a season in my life where I learned to be comfortable in my own skin. This did not mean that I preached on the seer anointing every week. I don't think I actually preached a single message on that topic. Instead, I began sharing some of the vision I'd had in prayer times leading up to the service. I began cautiously, as most seers usually do in unsure settings. The position I held in the ministry made it easy to steer the course in a direction that was favorable toward seers, but the environment wasn't exactly a hotbed for finding others with the same gifting. There was only ever one other seer in our midst, and she was just beginning to understand the gift. Learning to disciple another seer was incredibly valuable, but I wasn't in a vibrant prophetic community of seers.

It wasn't until our journey took us to Bethel that I encountered other seers. They weren't exactly coming out of the woodwork (I only met a few), but the environment actually allowed me to begin sharing more and more about my history with God and the things I'd seen and experienced in the Kingdom. More than that, the people I shared with were supportive and hungry to see this particular anointing expressed. From leaders to fellow students, everyone just wanted more of God. A great turning point was "outing" myself as a seer during a pre-trip meeting before a missions trip. We were doing a really simple ice breaker where we went around the group of thirty or so and introduced ourselves in one minute or less. I found myself saying I was a seer in the midst of my introduction. As the introductions continued, another guy named Matheus (who is now a friend) said, "Aaron and I, we are the same. I am a seer as well." After the meeting, another person came up and admitted she was a seer and wanted to spend some time talking about the gift. This was the beginning of my joining forces with a group of fellow seers at Bethel, which was also the start of a discipleship journey that changed my life.

It was the questions that people had about the seer anointing that were the seeds of this book. Somewhere between my own journey and operating in a gift of wisdom from the Father, I was answering questions that I had never even asked myself. It built my confidence to teach others about the gift, not just to have some answers, but to see the fruit in the lives of those around me as people began to walk in the seer anointing. In this season, I followed the Lord's leading in starting a YouTube channel to post videos about different topics relating to charismatic Christianity. It wasn't long before fellow students at BSSM began to stop me in the hallways to tell me they had watched a video about the seer anointing and felt that it made a huge part of their life make sense. They were beginning to feel comfortable in their skin, just like I had a few years before!

The days of seers living cloistered in caves and monasteries are long over. I remember one day, when ministry was particularly difficult, telling a friend I just wanted to live like a monk on a hill with Jesus. He looked at me like I'd grown a third eye. I realize now that I had been living that way when it came to my gift. I was safe and comfortable, but not bearing much fruit or fulfilling my destiny. I had to come out of my cave and into relationship and community to see growth and breakthrough come into the lives of the people around me. Using my gifts in public instead of private started to yield incredible fruit of healing, deliverance, and freedom in the lives of the people I served.

This is the time for seers to come out of the wilderness. The exodus has already begun. It is not a matter of whether they *will* impact the Church, but *when* and to what degree. Just look at what has happened in the Church as we've begun to once again embrace apostles and prophets into the fold! It happens without fail. When the seers are allowed their place, the same sort of increase will no doubt follow. This shift has been a long time coming and it should bring a grand sort of excitement to the Christian world. Prodigals are coming home and people are stepping into their prophetic destiny. This is cause for celebration!

Spiritual leaders must allow this transition to take place. The overarching approach to prophets, seers, and mystics has been one of trepidation and mistrust for far too long. We must use discernment, to be sure, but err on the side of grace. As seers come out of the wilderness and into community they must be accepted for who they are and be given an open door to walk in the gifts God has given them.

At the same time, seers push past the fear and accusation of the enemy and step into a place of openness regarding their gifts and talents. The devil only attacks valuable targets. You are valuable and your gift is valuable. Do not allow the enemy to take one more inch of ground by keeping you silent! Your silence is victory for him, so speak up and be heard; stand up and be counted. The more you get to be "you," the less the enemy will have the opportunity to steal from you and keep you in a place of shame, guilt, and inefficacy. Your greatest victory will start with allowing yourself the same thing that I was allowed; to be "me" in all the glory and honesty that God intended at creation.

SEERS AND THE FIVEFOLD MINISTRY

While it's true that most seers will probably have a bent toward the prophetic realm, placing limits on the working of the Holy Spirit in the lives of individuals is never a sound bet. The Fivefold Ministry is a concept that has been blessing the Church and supernatural culture for many years. If you don't understand the concept, or if it's new and foreign to you I would recommend tracking down some books and quality teaching that are dedicated to this topic.

In a nutshell, the Fivefold model correctly applies Ephesians 4:11-12, which states "And He gave some as apostles, and some as prophets, and some as evangelists, and some as pastors and teachers, for the equipping of the saints for the work of service, to the building up of the body of Christ." These roles are described as *offices* rather than *gifts*. An office doesn't mean a higher level of gifting; it means more responsibility. In a very real way, the offices are focused on making the Body more able and proficient in their individual gifts. They build the Church.

I remember having a great struggle with my identity at one point, mainly because I'd been told that I was three different offices by many different prophetic people in my sphere. It was confusion on a grand scale! Over time, I learned that the way we minister can be influenced by those receiving ministry. There are a few groups of people in my life that receive me as an apostle, and I flow in an apostolic anointing when I'm around them. There are some that receive me as a prophet, and I flow in a powerful prophetic anointing when around them. Both groups also receive me as a teacher of sorts. This is because offices are automatically called to teach and equip. A father of mine in the faith made that very clear to me while I was undergoing my identity crisis. Part of building up and equipping the church is teaching! You will not meet a true Fivefold apostle, prophet, teacher, evangelist, or pastor that isn't also a teacher to some degree! Fivefold teachers are some of my favorite people, just because they seem to so live and breathe their calling that it's hard not to step into revelation and a greater love of the Word when you're around them! It's almost like they have a double dose of the teacher anointing.

The seer is not an office, especially since we see a clear differentiation between seers and prophets in the Old Testament. Not all seers are prophets, and not all prophets are seers! I think that seers have a definite bent toward the office of a prophet, but I know just as many who don't have the slightest inkling toward that office. The gift does add to the function of every Fivefold office, and the interplay between an office call and the seer anointing are a dynamite combination. It is these potential blends of power and anointing that fill me with a profound hope for the seasons to come.

A teacher/seer has the potential to be at the fore of revival apologetics. These will not only experience the Kingdom with physical eyes, but couple their knowledge with their anointing and renewed mind to make the experiences make sense to others. Those with a teacher bent need Fivefold teachers to make experience "legal" from a scriptural and theological standpoint. Teachers are a bit like the ballast in a ship. They keep the ship from blowing over and sinking, but a ship that just had a ballast wouldn't go anywhere. A teacher with prophetic gifting still needs community, but they have a healthy amount of the supernatural to keep them moving closer to God and not closer to religion. The breath of God is wind in the sails for the teacher, but they are in little danger of blowing over because of their firm foundation. I believe God is raising up many prophet/teachers in this season and the teacher/seer is not left out of that movement. Teachers are like modern-day scribes, scouring the Word for new gems to reveal to the world. Seers look for the same things in the spiritual realm. Those two can come together in a glorious swirl that will advance the Kingdom!

To continue the ship analogy, pastors would be the sick bay. They are focused, in a powerful way, on making people feel safe and heard. They want to heal hurts above all else. Most healing "evangelists" I know are really pastors at heart; they just find the most success taking their healing ministry to the highways and byways. Fivefold pastors are not only incredible ministers, but they have a focus on training others to flow in pastoral ministry. My wife is a Fivefold pastor, and she has taught me to be more pastoral in my approach! My undergraduate studies were in pastoral ministry with a focus in counseling. I remember the lessons well. Poking and prodding and asking questions until we got to the root of the issue at hand. Most times I could see the root issue all over the person the second they walked in the door, but my training didn't leave room for words of knowledge and prophetic ministry. I was supposed to get them to say what their problem was because that would bring some level of self-awareness, or something like that.

The pastor/seer can dig to the root of the issue faster and begin the process of healing quicker than the conventional method I was taught. They will still feel compelled to climb down into the mud with those who are suffering, but the risk of codependency is lessened because the underlying issues will be plain to them. I believe a pastor/seer can develop a method for discerning the root causes in pain that can be taught to people who do not walk in the seer anointing. One should be mindful that they do not reduce God's work down to a formula (which often causes Him to do something different!), but understand that general revelation can help to break apart the enemy's foothold more quickly. There is also breakthrough available in partnering with the angelic realm. Pastor/seers will see more people healed because they understand the way the spiritual realm assists in our ministry efforts.

Evangelist/seers get me excited, plain and simple. As a seer, I have been a part of "treasure hunt" evangelism teams on the streets and it was a blast. For too long, evangelism has been reduced to trite formulas. Most true Fivefold evangelists understand this. Evangelists equip the Church to do the work of evangelism, but they must teach every believer to bring their personality and gifts to the table in order for their work to have maximum effect. They are like the rescue boat, constantly going out to save the survivors from the icy waters of the world. The evangelist/seer can literally see the strengths and gifts in the people they are equipping. They can then partner with the Holy Spirit to discover wisdom-infused strategies to successfully deploy them and draw in the harvest! As a seer, my approach to evangelism involves using my gift to create opportunities to encourage people and draw them into an encounter with God. Without fail, I will see a vision or see into the Spirit and use that information to break down the walls of the person in front of me.

Seer-evangelists will develop new Spirit-inspired strategies to invite people into encounters with Jesus. They will use every resource to make the Kingdom "real" for the one. I dream of a future where evangelists will look for the lost sheep caught up in the Occult and New Age movements and draw them back to their authentic identity as seers and prophetic people in the family of God! These gifted evangelists may be on the front lines of the battle more than ever, and they are more effective than ever when they partner with the Holy Spirit and lay aside their formulas.

Apostles benefit from the prophetic at every turn, with most apostles either carrying a strong prophetic gift or drawing prophets to themselves for relationship, guidance, and direction. An apostle who walks in the seer anointing doesn't suddenly slough off the need for these things. They do, however, come into a unique position to build a culture that values the mystical side of Christianity. If apostles are the builders of the ministry (not just visionary church planters, but long-range architects of Kingdom legacy), seer-apostles will infuse the spiritual realm into the very mortar of whatever they are currently building! We've used the phrase, "it's in the water" to describe negative situations for a long time (for example, limiting women in ministry is just "in the water"—as in most people naturally think in those terms because of the larger culture) but apostles who walk in the seer anointing can turn this into a positive situation. The supernatural can be "in the water" and become a part of our standard operating procedure. Apostles are like the wheelhouse and rudder of our ship. They can guide the culture of a house into a place that accepts and embraces the seer anointing.

Apostle/seers will shift the culture of the Church in a way that makes room for seers without downplaying the role of other gifts or generating a sense of spiritual elitism. They have a way of making people hungry for more of God. They can and will make the seer anointing they walk in available to a generation of believers!

Prophets have a mandate to equip the Church to hear the voice of God. They love nothing more than seeing others have their first vision, dream, word of knowledge, or encounter with God. They respond to most issues of today with, "We just need to hear God more, and more clearly." They are the sails of the great ship that is the Church, catching the breath of God and propelling the vessel forward.

Prophet/seers are opportunely positioned to see others step into the seer anointing. Their anointing is already one that makes it easier for people to experience the prophetic. They extend this mandate to the physical eyes of those in their sphere. They are the ones who will develop new strategies and methods to open the eyes of a generation.

The Fivefold Ministry is the most biblical model of church government that we have at our disposal today, and the seer anointing can bring much to the table. Even though "seer" isn't an office in the Church, it's still a gift that every believer should desire—none more than our apostles, prophets, teachers, pastors, and evangelists.

CHAPTER 7

THE FUTURE FOR SEERS

It is an understatement to say that the future for seers is a bright one. The call has gone out from heaven to restore the seer anointing to a place of honor and prominence in the Kingdom. Remember, we aren't talking about elevating seers above those who possess other spiritual gifts, we are walking out a healthy restoration of the seer anointing in the Church today. The Body has functioned without this critical component for far too long, as every part is critical! When seers are restored to the Church, revelation can only become more common and more vivid. I believe that seers carry a unique revelation of the fabric of heaven. As this revelation spreads, awareness of the Kingdom grows with it. This advancement means a few things, not the least of which being more seers coming into the ranks of the Church both from inside and outside the four walls. It will also result in an increase in the prophetic realm and the gift of faith within a spiritual community. Seers are prophetic in nature, and much of the seer's function undergirds prophetic culture. A Kingdom culture that includes seers in the prophetic milieu will be even more vivid and life-giving than what we have seen, which is saying something!

There's something about the seer that bolsters faith in the people of their community. It's not just the seer that gets to see the fruit of their vision; those around them get to see it as well. Seeing into the heavens dispels the spirit of unbelief and ensures the only doubt present is a healthy doubt that leads people into a deeper level of faith. This acceleration of faith brings about miracles, signs, and wonders! When seers are accepted and plugged back into the Body more healings will take place, more demons will be cast out, more angelic activity will occur, and more souls will come into the Kingdom! The potential fruit is nearly endless.

In our personal lives, the key to productivity is health. Healthy people are almost always productive people. Turning people into "producers" without making them healthy in every area of their lives only generates a culture of burnout and high turnover. The same can be applied to the Body of Christ. If the Body is healthy, every function happens smoothly and without incident. People hear from God, are healed and delivered, souls are saved, and culture is impacted and shaped. If the Body is in disrepair (missing a part, for instance), these functions still work to some extent, but they don't reach their full potential. Think of it like twisting or spraining an ankle. While it's possible to walk, work, and do almost every function required, some movements are just more difficult or uncomfortable than others. Life is just easier when your body is in proper working order. In the same way, the Kingdom walk is easier when the Body is functioning at full capacity.

As seers rise up and come out of the proverbial wilderness we will see an unfathomable season of great acceleration touch the Church. In the prophetic realm, it's almost as though the seers are the reinforcements we have been praying for and calling forth for so long. The restoration of the seers is like the arrival of the cavalry! We long for an increase in heavenly activity and for a richer experience of

God's Presence. The seers present an open door to this reality. As they are given permission to take their place we will begin to experience greater degrees of God's presence and supernatural activity. This isn't *just* because of the seer anointing, it's because God is taking us "from glory to glory" as He has promised. That alone should spark a vision of the future that is filled with hope and optimism.

To vision cast a bit, I dream of this coming reality not just for my own sake, but for the sake of my daughter. I imagine a future where her gift can be expressed freely and valued by the Church at large. She should be free to be herself, even if that means having visions of heaven and seeing into the spiritual realm. I want her to have even more freedom than I have to share her experience, and to feel that what she is seeing is valid and worthy to be shared. I want what she sees to "pull back the veil" for people to see God more clearly, so they may be invited in to His Kingdom work.

A NEW STEP OF FAITH

There is acceleration in the gift of faith that goes along with the seer anointing. This looks like taking the risk of allowing a healthy dose of mystery back into the equation. We have somehow believed the lie that faith means we have no evidence of our belief. We've so tipped the scale in the favor of mystery that the healthy balance has been lost in many circles. "Blind faith" isn't faith at all, but gullibility. The more a person experiences God, the more their faith grows and the more they realize they *don't* understand. This creates a need for mystery rather than allowing mystery in as a crutch, an easy answer for hard questions. Anyone who believes they have God figured out has stopped growing and stopped walking in relationship with Him. There isn't a person alive who would seriously claim to have the Eternal sorted out, but there is an attitude floating around right now that certainly functions like theological knowledge is equivalent to actual relationship.)Being able to explain every circumstance and situation is a sad shadow of a substitute for really knowing the Father. It is as damaging as blind faith. Both are faithless extremes, one because everything is called "faith" and the other because nothing qualifies.

There is no greater example of this than the book of Job. Remember, many scholars still disagree on whether Job is an actual account or a play written to illustrate the nature of God (or any other number of interpretations). Job is usually the first piece of evidence referenced by a person who is trying to put the goodness of God on trial. I am the absolute last person to downplay the grief and loss associated with the sorts of things Job experienced, but from a purely empirical standpoint, Job experienced all of the terrible things the scriptural account highlights over the course of a single year. Job had all of his theological ducks in a row. He was flawless in his defense of who he thought God was, and on his judgement of his own innocence. Job had removed mystery from the equation, in the same way many denominations and theologians strive to do today.

Suddenly, everything changed. Job had an experience that grew his faith and taught Him about the real nature of God. This experience did not come from embracing suffering, from hearing a great sermon preached, or from coming into a place of greater theological understanding. Instead, Job *saw* God. The book of Job asks more questions of God than it answers, but the climax of the story is this incredible account of how seeing God changed Job's perspective: "I have heard of You by the hearing of the ear; but now my eye sees You; therefore I retract, and I repent in dust and ashes" (Job 42:5-6).

Job had *heard* about God, but *seeing* God turned all of his theology to dust and reframed his experience. Job saw, and suddenly the mystery was returned to his understanding of God. The Kingdom became bigger for Job, not smaller. God had broken out of the box of

Job's intellect and reasoning. Face-to-face with the Almighty, the only thing Job could do was change his mind. He was forced to return to the drawing board, and he had *seen* God!

Generally, people who lack faith will say things like, "If I could just see God, if I could just know that He is real, I would believe." Job saw God and had to rethink everything he had previously believed about God. This experience didn't answer all of his questions but in fact generated more questions. Job lived the rest of his life with a new understanding of just how *little* he understood God. But he also lived in prosperity and in a deeper relationship with Him. When Job let go of his own defenses, his theological boxes, and his preconceived notions about his situation, he found himself in the Presence of the Divine.

Faith is easier to walk out when you've seen God, or even seen His angels. It doesn't negate faith to have the experiences that many seers have; it actually generates a new level of faith. Seeing into the spiritual realm keeps us asking questions of God and keeps us in a place of being dependent upon Him. Many people are asking questions that can only be adequately answered by an encounter with God. Anything else is a disservice to them. As the seer anointing is openly shared and spread, many more people will have their face-to-face encounter with God. I can attest personally to the fact that this sort of encounter changes you. Whether it happens once in your lifetime, or on many occasions, a face-to-face encounter with God will leave one forever changed.

This is a faith revolution. Any doubts about the goodness of God fade away in His presence. Moving past these questions does not dispel all doubt, but it does open one up to a whole new slew of questions and causes them to embark on a new journey with God. It is almost as though we go from asking, "Is there a God?" to "Who is God?" We can answer the old question, "Is God for me?" and move on to "What is my role alongside the Creator of the Universe?" Our faith becomes deeper as our relationship with Jesus grows more intimate. If our experiences cause us to sing "God is good!" at every turn, the possibilities of what He can do in us and through us become literally endless. Every door we previously thought was open only to the spiritual elite or the theologically educated suddenly becomes accessible.

Imagine a generation that doesn't have to grapple with the question of God's existence before they can give themselves over to healing ministry. Imagine all of the roadblocks and detours on the road to destiny fade away in one encounter with the Father. That is what an increase in the gift of faith offers the Church today, and the seer anointing provides an access point to this increase. Faith and mystery are engaged in the dance of the ages, and this dance circles deeper and deeper. As we see more of God, we long to see even more of Him. As we stumble upon more mysteries, we ponder and pray to understand and just when we think we've been filled to the breaking point, God opens up a whole new facet of His being and we are overwhelmed all over again. This is the journey of faith.

FROM GLORY TO GLORY

The phrase "glory to glory" comes from 2 Corinthians 3:18, and it is less an opportunity and more a description of the process that every believer steps into the moment they believe. We are being transformed into the likeness of Christ, from glory to glory. I believe the restoration of the seer anointing is one of these steps to glory. The Bride and Christ are in this sort of cyclical dance, one that has been going on throughout the ages. God is leading us all into a closer relationship with Himself, and a more intimate place of dependency and revelation. As each of us pursue God and all that He has, we find ourselves becoming His perfect bride. And so, we all partake in the dance.

This looks like vulnerability, transparency, and integration of your gifts, talents, anointing, and everything you love. I have seen so much more of Christ (and more miracles, signs, and wonders) since I began being honest about who I am and what I see. It has been the single biggest step in my own personal process of going from glory to glory. My challenge to you is this: Will you join me in this messy, tear-filled, yet unstoppably wonderful dance?

Let me be clear: walking this way is messy and raw, but so is revival. There may be setbacks, missteps, and even rejection at times, but it is all worth it when compared to the wonderful destiny available to those who are willing to choose the way of intimacy with the Father. The more we step into our identity, the more revival can flow through us and change our churches, cities, and nations. As we pray for revival, let us realize that we ourselves *are* revival!

Do not despise the day of small beginnings. The breakthrough you've been praying for just might begin with a revelation of the depth of who God has created you to be. If that is the small key that opens the big door for your region, you owe it to yourself and those in your sphere to be vulnerable. I will never forget an experience I had on a mission trip just after our season at Bethel came to an end. We were debriefing as a team on the back end of a week of extraordinary ministry and encounters with God. We were going around the circle, sharing what had impacted us the most. I'd seen God do some incredible things and gotten to be a part of encouraging, commissioning, and healing many individuals.

As I half listened and half planned what I was going to say, the Holy Spirit gave me a profound vision of my first-year Revival Group Pastor, Angela, telling our group that the word "vulnerable" was taken from the Latin word "*vulna*" which means "to wound."

In that moment, I knew what God was asking of me. This wasn't the time to brag, even if my boasting was in Christ and His riches. It was a group that needed me to bare my heart, as much as I needed to share my process. I opened up, sharing my difficulties through tears about the most profound thing that had happened to me. I had heard one of the local ministers ask pastors to come forward. This was the first time I'd heard something along this line and remained in my seat. When we left for California, I had laid down the church in Wisconsin, which I had pastored for ten years, and never grieved the transition. Instead, I had buried it in every way that I could. That moment of vulnerability allowed me to begin a healthy (and long overdue) process of grieving, which I did not have to walk through alone. One of the surprising side effects of vulnerability is it creates fresh avenues and opportunities for support.

Going from glory to glory doesn't always look clean and perfect. It is real, alive, messy, and sometimes painful, but the holiness of the seasons is enough to keep us chasing the Presence. I invite all of you seers and anyone who is hungry to step into the supernatural to join in the Divine dance. Push past the voices that attempt to keep you in isolation, knowing that the Body of Christ needs what you carry. You may even be surprised to find others just like you, hungering for the next great move of the Spirit.

BIBLIOGRAPHY

Bentley, G. (1969). *Blake Records.* Oxford: Clarendon Press.

Bentley, G. (1975). *William Blake: The Critical Heritage.* London: Routledge and Kegan Paul, Inc. .

Kowalska, M. F. (2005). *Diary of Saint Maria Faustina Kowalska: Divine Mercy in My Soul.* Stockbridge, MA: Marian Press.

Lewis, C. (2001). *The Screwtape Letters.* San Francisco: HarperCollins.

WSInt. (2014). *Akiane.* Retrieved August 11, 2015, from https://www.akiane.com/about

ABOUT THE AUTHOR

 **Aaron J. Peterson** began hearing the voice of God and walking in the supernatural at a young age. He has been pastoring, training, and equipping believers for supernatural ministry since planting his first church at the age of eighteen with his wife, Cally. Aaron holds a master's degree from Crown College and is a graduate of the Bethel School of Supernatural Ministry. His academic training and supernatural experience lend to an approach that successfully balances theology and Charismatic expression. Today, Aaron and Cally serve at Elevation Church in Green Bay, Wisconsin, where they lead the Elevate U School of Supernatural Ministry.

Made in the USA
Middletown, DE
11 December 2019